PRAISE FOR *THE GUIDED JOURNEY*!

"Great stories, great applications, and a working manual for life! Mike Lee has laid out a proven process for discovering your purpose in life. His perspective as a strategy consultant, business leader, family man, and person of faith make his advice practical for anyone seeking direction and inspiration in life. My hope is that this gets into many people's hands and becomes a gift that can be shared for generations."

Frank Harrison
Chair and CEO Coca-Cola Consolidated and Founder of T-Factor

"Mike has applied strategic-planning concepts, honed from his work over thirty years in consulting to companies and organizations, and applied them to strategic planning for your life. Just as he has helped companies envision where they want to go and plan practical steps to get there, he has laid out a proven process to help envision your future and help you get there. This is [illegible]."

Harsha V. Agadi
[illegible]ent and CEO Crawford & Company

"[illegible] urpose. *The Guided Journey* is filled with practical and powerful applications that will help push the reset button on our life perspective. Mike weaves in rich story-telling with real life principles that he's learned over his storybook career. Bring a pen and highlighter along for this one, and enjoy the ride!"

Dave Alpern
President of 4-Time NASCAR Champion Joe Gibbs Racing

"I was privileged to read an early copy of *The Guided Journey*. Once I started, I could not put this book down. Not only because of the advice offered for how to find your purpose, but also because Mike gives us a real look into what a God-centered life looks like. Mike is an authentic role model, and I would recommend this book to people in all stages of life, especially young men."

Jennifer McCormick King

Former Bank of America Executive and single Mom

"*The Guided Journey* is a practical guide to living a purpose-driven life. Mike shares personal and professional stories to illustrate how to make thoughtful, purposeful choices. These examples provide a roadmap of how to deal with obstacles and experience joy in your life."

Bob Hull

Founder of Integrity Strategic Solutions
and former CFO of Lowe's Companies, Inc.

"What Mike Lee has learned and shares in *The Guided Journey* is that there is a spiritual dimension, a God-guided direction and dimension to all of life, including family, personal life, and business, sometimes referred to as our calling—if we only recognize and allow God's intimate involvement. Allowing that spiritual partnership with him and others brings passionate purpose, meaning, and abundantly fulfilling success. I heartily recommend the reading of this practical work."

Tom Phillips

Vice- President, Billy Graham Evangelistic Association

"I have had so many people ask me about having purpose in their career and in life. *The Guided Journey* is a must read for everyone in search of purpose. Mike shares his story, lessons learned, practical tips, and a process to find purpose and joy in life."

Mark Linsz

Former Treasurer Bank of America
and Co-Founder My Next Season

The Guided Journey

The Guided JOURNEY

Finding Faith, Purpose, and Joy in Life

NEW YORK

LONDON • NASHVILLE • MELBOURNE • VANCOUVER

The Guided Journey

Finding Faith, Purpose, and Joy in Life

© 2020 Mike G. Lee

All rights reserved. No portion of this book may be reproduced, stored in a retrieval system, or transmitted in any form or by any means—electronic, mechanical, photocopy, recording, scanning, or other—except for brief quotations in critical reviews or articles, without the prior written permission of the publisher.

Published in New York, New York, by Morgan James Publishing. Morgan James is a trademark of Morgan James, LLC. www.MorganJamesPublishing.com

ISBN 9781642795387 paperback
ISBN 9781642795394 eBook
Library of Congress Control Number: 2019937660

Cover Design by:
Megan Dillon
megan@creativeninjadesigns.com

Interior Design by:
Chris Treccani
www.3dogcreative.net

Morgan James PUBLISHING
Builds
with...
Habitat for Humanity®
Peninsula and Greater Williamsburg

Morgan James is a proud partner of Habitat for Humanity Peninsula and Greater Williamsburg. Partners in building since 2006.

Get involved today! Visit
MorganJamesPublishing.com/giving-back

To Kelli, my best friend and wife:
You are the light of my life.

To my dear children, Alex, Cami, and Olivia:
Always know I love you to the moon and back.

To my mom, dad, and sisters:
Though we live apart, know that I love you very much.

To my grandparents:
Thank you for the foundation of faith, your courage,
and perseverance.

To my customers, friends, and colleagues:
Thank you for your trust and inspiration—and
for challenging me.

To God:
Thank you for my mind, each breath, each heartbeat,
and for loving us all so unconditionally.

CONTENTS

Part One:
The Burning Platform

The Moment I Realized
I Needed to Make a Change

CHAPTER 1

The Enron and Arthur Andersen Explosion

We all remember where we were the morning of September 11, 2001. I was in my Arthur Andersen Business Consulting office in uptown Charlotte that day when a coworker frantically came in my office and said, "Oh, my gosh, turn on the news! It looks like a plane crashed into one of the twin towers in New York City!"

We all tried to get on CNN.com to see what was happening, but the website was down with so many people trying to get information. We would later learn it was a terrorist attack. All our employees were sent home for the day as there was the concern that other skyscrapers might be hit. I remember working with my wife, Kelli, to get our son, Alex, home from elementary school; he was in kindergarten at the time and old enough to remember and comprehend what happened that day. Thousands of Americans' lives were changed when nearly 3,000 of their loved ones died in that terrorist attack.

What I didn't know was that my life would soon change as Arthur Andersen was hit and destroyed by its association with Enron and that company's accounting practices. This investigation did not kill a family member or harm my life for many years, but it did force me to evaluate my purpose in life.

I had joined the accounting firm, Arthur Andersen, in Charlotte, North Carolina, in the summer of 1990 after graduating from Virginia Tech with a bachelor's degree in business and a major in accounting. Kelli and I were married June 11, 1994, and with my newfound faith we were happy and ready to begin a new life together. At work I was digging into financial statements of companies from a wide variety of industries and getting a chance to work with very smart and motivated people. During these early years I was enjoying the consulting projects I was doing with big companies. I got satisfaction out of seeing positive change with my clients because of our work.

After three years with Arthur Andersen in their audit practice, I had the opportunity to move from auditing to consulting and strategic planning. This was when I realized how much I loved strategic work—envisioning a new future—and then building a plan to accomplish it. I was finding my passion on the right (creative and strategic) side of my brain.

In 2000 we sold a huge project to Sara Lee doing global, shared-services strategy and execution. I got the news, "Congratulations, you've been promoted to partner." I had worked with Arthur Andersen for eleven years, and this was an incredible career milestone, which promised a higher income, albeit with more responsibility and continued travel.

Yet looking back, I had the nagging feeling that things were out of balance. Kelli had always supported my career, and we were in it together always, but I could see that she was struggling with my extensive travel, my intense work schedule, and two young kids. Thankfully, we couldn't see the iceberg looming on the horizon.

A month after 9/11 on October 22, 2001 an investigation was announced into improper accounting practices at Enron Corporation, one of Arthur Andersen's largest clients. I literally had the paperwork for admittance into the partnership on my desk and was ready to take out a $100,000 loan to buy into the firm. Even then I had a sick, uneasy feeling about everything, but didn't think there was any way the firm would go down.

A good friend asked me, "Mike, I saw what is happening with Enron and Arthur Andersen today on CNN. You don't think your company could go out of business, do you?"

"No way," I said. "They will settle."

Boy, was I wrong.

That is why it was so ironic a few months later around the holidays when we all got the email that said, "Heads up, this Enron situation could be serious."

Over the next several months it became clear that Arthur Andersen would not survive. At the time I was upset about the timing, thinking it was cruelly ironic. In hindsight, the timing worked out for me, as I had not been admitted into the partnership and therefore was free of liability. We were getting updates from the senior leadership of Arthur Andersen on a regular basis via our global voicemail system. For several months they put up a good fight with the government, hoping to settle the issue, take a fine, and return things to normal.

At the time I was thankful to have the distraction of a big project with a private company, Morris Communications. My team was lucky, because many of Arthur Andersen's large public clients were dropping Andersen as their auditor, and Morris remained with us. The paperwork for my admittance to the partnership sat unsigned on my desk in Charlotte while I worked full time in Augusta, Georgia, with Morris Communications. We had about twenty-five consultants working there to architect and implement a new finance, human resources, and information technology organization, all these processes on a world-class system called SAP. (SAP is an Enterprise Resource Planning system engineered by a German company and can have a dramatic and positive impact on the way a company operates more efficiently, with better information to run its business.)

SAP needs to be implemented well, to exact specifications. Done poorly it could sink a company. Our client Morris Communications and the family that owns them were counting on us to do this right, and the future of their company was riding on it. The members of the Morris family are honest, hardworking people who had put their trust in us—and specifically in me. This had been my first attempt as a newly promoted partner to sell and deliver a project with little supervision from my more senior partner; let's call him Tim. I took this responsibility and the millions of dollars they were investing with us very seriously. The weight of getting it done right was significant and a lot to handle for a thirty-three year-old. I also had twenty-five people working for me that expected my day-to-day leadership on the project and my calm reassurance that things would work out okay for the firm.

During this stressful time I was working Monday through Thursday away from my young family. Alex was six years old and Cami was three. Kelli had her hands full at home during the week, and I would try to do my best to be a great dad and husband Friday to Sunday, attempting to make up for my absence. We were both excited that I had made partner, but we were very anxious to see where the Enron situation would end.

It was in this uncertain period in March of 2002, that Kelli and I got the great news that she was pregnant with our third child, Olivia. We were so excited to be having a baby since we had always dreamed of having three children. As happy as I was about this news, the stress of working twelve-to-fourteen hour days for my client, supervising my team, and dealing with the uncertainty of the Enron scandal, was becoming too much. I was also starting to realize that the sustainability of traveling every week with two young children and a third on the way was going to be an issue. Kelli was not telling me to make changes, but I was sensing this work/life/family balance just didn't compute.

Just when I thought things couldn't get more stressful, I got a phone call from my dad, "Mike, Arthur Andersen has been indicted. It doesn't look like they will be able to do audits anymore."

I'm not claiming to be a rocket scientist on this one as I felt naïve for hoping that it would all work out for the firm, but I now knew Arthur Andersen would go out of business. Over the next few days firm leadership was privately contemplating what options they had as they desperately tried to change the government's mind.

It all happened very quickly. From October 22, 2001, when the investigation into Arthur Andersen's role in the Enron accounting scandal was announced, to the June 15, 2002 conviction of Arthur Andersen for obstruction of justice, the firm's publicly-traded clients were defecting in large numbers. Clients who were privately held stuck with Arthur Andersen a little longer, but we all knew it was just a matter of time until the firm failed. April to June was one of the craziest time periods in my business and family life.

I had a lot of priorities and commitments to consider. We had a client that was halfway into a major project, and I felt a tremendous sense of responsibility to deliver for them and their people. Tim and I had about fifty people whom we were responsible for. I had the twenty-five people who were working with me on Morris in Augusta, Georgia, and we had another twenty-five across several other clients. I also had to think about my wife, Kelli, my two children, and our new baby on the way and how I would provide for them. The weight of that responsibility was heavy, and I wanted to do everything I could to provide a path forward.

This three-month period became increasingly stressful and challenging. The partners were taking a huge financial hit and were exposed to significant legal action and liability. As in any disaster you see the best and the worst in people. When the Titanic sunk some passengers panicked and stepped over others to get into lifeboats; other people were heroes who risked their own lives to save fellow passengers. Thankfully our situation wasn't truly life and death, but it was a significant business disaster and we were living in the middle of it. Eighty-eight thousand people would be out of a job in three months. The ship was sinking.

This was a time when everyone impacted by this was forced to do a lot of self-reflection and think about what they wanted to do in the future. Where would we be working? Would we have to find another job quickly? My team at Morris Communications felt a little more secure because we had a private company as a client.

I discussed the situation with Steve Stone, the Chief Financial Officer of Morris Communications. Steve was a client we had worked with before, and we had recommended Morris hire him. He had moved his family to Augusta so he could work for Morris Communications and lead all the administrative functions we were building. I also spoke with Will Morris, Morris Communications

President, about the situation and our options. I was concerned that we would lose our team as everyone would start looking for new jobs, out of concern for their future.

Incredibly Morris Communications agreed to commit to put us all on their payroll to insure that we would complete the project. This commitment allowed us to keep the entire team together throughout the turmoil. Our business cards would change several times, but we stayed with Morris to completion.

During this very uncertain period, let me say again that Arthur Andersen's leadership did a very good job of communicating directly to us with almost daily updates. Partners in audit and consulting were being encouraged to find places for their teams to go. They were evaluating deals for parts of Arthur Andersen to be acquired piecemeal by the other "Big Four" or regional firms. Partners were asked to coordinate their activities with regional leadership, but they were not precluded from taking their practices and teams to other firms.

Any deal had to be reviewed by an internal committee that was set up to coordinate the "fire sale." Because I was a new partner and because I was 100 percent focused on working for my client, I was not privy to deals that were being evaluated at the firm-wide level. I was only involved in the deals that Tim and the other regional consulting partners were considering. Because I was the most junior partner and because I was willing to work extra hours on the financial analyses, I did the heavy lifting on the presentations our team built as "pitch decks" (specific pitches) to potential investors/acquirers. This extra work, along with the long hours on my regular client work at Morris, made this the busiest couple of months of my life. I was now routinely putting in eighteen-to-twenty-hour days.

This was one of the moments when I realized I needed to make a change. I call such times "Burning Platforms," a term from my consulting work with clients. It is a metaphor used to describe the case for making changes in an organization. The idea is that you need to articulate the clear rationale for an individual or group to change what they are doing and move in a different direction. If the platform isn't burning, people won't feel the heat and move off the platform they are on.

You might be in a moment somewhat like this. You are not happy, not feeling fulfilled, not motivated, and having a hard time getting out of bed in the mornings. You dread Sunday afternoons as you prepare for the work week. It could be you are experiencing difficult circumstances: a death in the family, a sick child, your own health issues. It could be you have been laid off or fired. Whatever the circumstances, you are in a situation where you need to reevaluate what you are doing. This doesn't mean you need to drop everything and quit your job, but you need to take a step back, evaluate where you are going, and consider what changes you need to make. One of the biggest risks to anyone in transition is not with finding a job; it is accepting a job too soon that is off-purpose.

Or you might be just graduating from college and looking for a job. Or even in college and considering a change in your major. All of us look for a purposeful future.

In this book I will lay out a proven, eleven-step process for building a purpose-led life. I used this process throughout my career as a management consultant for Arthur Andersen for thirteen years. And then as a major contributor to the growth of a work-life, balance-friendly consulting model with North Highland (the winner of seven, top-four consecutive awards for the Best Place to Work by *Consulting Magazine*). During my twelve years at North

Highland, company revenue grew from $48 million to over $400 million in total across twenty-five locations worldwide.

In 2015 I founded a new consulting company called Independence Consulting, focused on helping organizations define and realize long-term, sustainable strategies through a trademarked approach called Strategy Realized™. I have used this process with dozens of Fortune 500 clients where I have done strategic planning, cost and efficiency evaluation, and complex technology programs.

After an incredible three-and a-half-year experience starting our own company, my wife and I sold Independence Consulting to Point B, a several-hundred-million-dollar, employee-owned management consulting company. Our whole team joined Point B, because they were the one consulting company we knew of who shared a similar culture and set of values.

Consulting has been my calling and business my mission field for more than twenty-eight years.

Throughout that time I have helped companies identify how they can become more profitable on a sustainable basis. Sometimes when analyzing the root cause of internal financial bleeding, we explore overlooked areas for a wound site. Once found we stop the hemorrhaging and bind up the wound. This is necessary for the financial health of the business in order to keep it alive, thriving, and prosperous for its people and its contribution to society. Then we look for growth areas to help the company flourish and make its mark. In many ways companies are like people. Sometimes our hearts hemorrhage and need to be healed due to the stresses of life, unfortunate events, and poor choices.

At moments like these, clients will come to me after my professional work with them and ask for personal advice on a job change or how to solve a particular problem. That's when I've used the process in this book over and over again. One very high-profile client called me specifically to thank me for walking him through this process. He was an executive of a Fortune 500 company that had just restructured and he was leaving through no fault of his own.

This executive had followed my advice to think through his Life Purpose Statement and his Role Success Statements. He said, "For the first time in our adult lives my wife and I are talking about where we want to be and what we want to be doing before looking at job opportunities. I can't tell you how much I appreciate your advice. It means a lot to us." His response to this process is typical of the response I've received from many.

Throughout this book we will explore this eleven-step process and the twists and turns life can throw at us—and how to not only stay on track but to experience joy in the high points, low points, and the steady moments. We will look at how to get back on target when life and/or our own mistakes throw us off track. I will also share my own personal story as I journeyed through life using this process.

The Arthur Andersen twist was only one of many in my life. The next years had many twists and turns.

CHAPTER 2

Twists and Turns during the Andersen Fire Sale

During this difficult period when the Andersen "fire sale" was occurring, I got a phone call from a guy named Scott Evans, a recruiter for an entrepreneurial, start-up consulting firm called North Highland; they were looking to expand into Charlotte from Atlanta. (I would later learn that the president of the company had received my name from an Arthur Andersen partner in Atlanta.) Scott was very persistent. He said, "Mike, with a wife and two kids and another on the way, you need to think about getting off the road, buddy." He connected me with their president who told me, "Mike, you can do the same, big-time client work you do now, you can work with big companies, focusing on building your client base in Charlotte—and be home to help raise your family."

I was intrigued by the idea of this but was skeptical at first. Why wouldn't everybody do that if it was possible? I took an afternoon off and went to visit North Highland in Atlanta to do my due-diligence. I thought it was wise to at least listen, given the situation at Andersen. I can be loyal to a fault, so this was the only opportunity I looked into.

Simultaneously with my visit to Atlanta we learned that Arthur Andersen had agreed to sell the United States Business Consulting Division, my unit, to BearingPoint Consulting. It was a last-minute deal but at least we had a home. This meant I'd have about four weeks to figure out whether to go with the team to BearingPoint Consulting, go to North Highland, or consider other options.

Because I was working so much and because I had the commitment from Morris to employ us, I did not consider other options. The North Highland option was interesting because of the promise of work/life family balance. They made me an offer on Monday of the week we had to leave Arthur Andersen by Friday, the day we would "check out." It was a very difficult decision and one that only Kelli and I discussed. We decided that we would accept the North Highland offer, because of the appeal of the work/life balance and being able to put my family first and still do the consulting work I love. I got North Highland to agree to let me make sure Morris Communications was going to approve of the plan. I was not going to leave them feeling abandoned after all they had done for us.

It was one of those defining moments in my life where I had to make a quick decision based on the information I had at the time. Once Kelli and I made the decision I made plans to talk with my partner Tim at Arthur Andersen since we were making final plans for the transition to BearingPoint Consulting the following Monday.

The initial conversation went fine that Tuesday morning, though Tim did try to talk me out of going to North Highland and indicated that the other partners wanted me to stay with them and go over to BearingPoint Consulting. I shared my desire to do consulting work in Charlotte so I could focus more time on my family during the week rather than time-consuming travel outside the city. Tim asked me to give the partners time to think about it and I agreed to give them the rest of the day.

Later that Tuesday evening I received a call. They really wanted me to go to BearingPoint Consulting with them and they were willing to offer me more money. I explained that it was not about money though I did appreciate the offer (that offer made me wonder if I was underpaid!). Again, they asked me for some more time, even though they could see I was firm in my decision. Out of respect for my twelve years with them I agreed to give it until Wednesday morning. It was now two days before our last day at Arthur Andersen.

What happened next was shocking. I got a call from Tim and the message was clear, though unbelievable. He said, "Mike, we want you to know that if you leave, we will not extend offer letters for your team to come to BearingPoint Consulting. We and the acquiring firm are considering this a per-partner hire (which meant that BearingPoint was only agreeing to hire my team if I came over with them), and even though you aren't legally a partner yet, we are considering you a partner for the deal. On the positive side we can commit to promoting you to the partner level after the deal closes, and we get everyone over there."

I was disappointed and shocked with the tactics. Tim knew, and I knew, that he and members of my team could easily step in and do the client work that I had going; there were several who knew exactly how to do it and I'd agreed to an orderly transition. I cannot be sure why this stipulation was added, but this seemed like blackmail. They knew me, and they knew I would never do that to my team. They couldn't get me with money, so they were going to get me by leveraging my integrity. Now it was my turn to ask them to give me the night to get back to them.

That Wednesday night it really didn't take Kelli and I long to discuss it. She asked me, "Do you think they are bluffing? They wouldn't really leave twenty-five people out of job, would they? Not when they are all billable on Morris. That doesn't make sense."

"Yes, I do think they are bluffing, but there is no time to figure this out. We must 'check out' of Arthur Andersen on Friday. I can't be certain that they are bluffing, and I won't put my colleagues at risk."

"I completely agree," Kelli replied.

"I guess we are going to have to go on to BearingPoint Consulting, get everybody over there, and then see where we go from there," I said.

"I'm with you 100 percent, Mike. I just can't believe they are doing this. It's just wrong!" Kelli exclaimed.

On Thursday morning, I reluctantly called Tim and told him I would be going over with my team on Monday. Looking back on it I'm pretty sure they felt smart at that point. They were forcing me to go against my will, using people's jobs as leverage.

My next call was to Dan Reardon, the then-president of North Highland, to tell him why I couldn't join at that time. He said, "Mike, I appreciate your telling me this and I understand the reason you are going to BearingPoint. Frankly, it makes me want you here even more. But you need to know that we can't wait around on you. We have to look for other options."

"I understand. I'm disappointed for myself and my family but you need to keep moving forward. I'm going to get things settled for everyone over there and then I hope we can talk again later."

"That sounds like a plan," Dan said.

I got off the phone, took a deep breath, and mentally decided to move on and make the best of it. We had work to do for Morris, and I could help get our team over to the new company. I felt good about doing the right thing. I could look myself in the mirror.

That Friday we "checked out" of Arthur Andersen. It was like checking out of a hotel, I guess. You turned in your laptop, your key, and you filled out your final expense report. And just like that I walked out of Arthur Andersen at the age of thirty-three, having been there twelve years. It was a sad day, seeing my only employer close its famous wooden doors for the last time. I drove home that Friday night ready to just relax and spend the weekend with my family and get mentally prepared to show up at BearingPoint Consulting on Monday morning. I was still consulting at Morris Communications so even though my business card changed from Arthur Andersen Business Consulting to BearingPoint Consulting my team and I would continue to do our day-to-day work at Morris.

That Monday morning when my team arrived at BearingPoint's office in uptown Charlotte, we all filed into a training room where a human-resources employee walked us through basic onboarding materials. It was an orderly, step-by-step process, cold and calculated. I felt as if we would next be pushed into some winding stalls like cattle and branded. I knew within ten minutes that I would not be with this firm any longer than needed. However, it was fine for now, because it gave us a way to serve Morris Communications and to keep our team together.

The first day in the BearingPoint offices after our "processing" was very strange. Most of the partners didn't even come by and say hello, literally staying in their offices. The good thing, though, is I did meet one amazing guy who is still a close friend to this day. As I set up my computer in my office, this guy knocked on the door and said, "Hey there, I'm Peter. I just wanted to come by and say hello and welcome you to the company. If you need anything or have any question, please don't hesitate to come see me." As he walked away, I was struck by his light in what seemed like darkness. Peter Wong had no reason to talk to any of us as we were assigned to a completely different team than the one he was on.

During that first year at BearingPoint Consulting a lot of former Arthur Andersen people were thinking about what they wanted to do next with their career. The trauma of the Andersen downfall and the ensuing mess had me seriously thinking about what God wanted me to do with the rest of my life. While I stayed focused on keeping the Morris project on track, I vacillated between considering other consulting jobs, industry positions, and even the ministry or missions work. You see I've had a passion for helping people and specifically children. It sounds broad, but it ranges from helping children around the world to caring for my own children. I guess you could say I was lost in the wilderness and I was looking for my compass.

I would do research. I would talk to people. Unfortunately I was treating this like a project that I was going to figure out on my own. This is the problem with earning your living as a "problem solver": every week I solve clients' problems. It is also an issue with a fact-based, CPA, analytical mind–always trying to figure out the answer on my own. I'm also a guy. That is what we often do as business leaders. We solve problems on our own. We don't need help.

Sure I would talk to Kelli about it, and she would try to help me but there was something missing. I would pray about it, but my prayers would be for specifics or direction. I wanted an answer, but I hadn't yet submitted to the Creator and given him control of this process. I wanted direction, but first he wanted submission to him.

During my eleven months at BearingPoint Consulting some good things did happen. We completed the architecture for the Morris work and established the project team of internal and external resources needed to successfully implement it. We were all gainfully employed for that year and none of us lost our jobs. We all eventually did leave over a one-to-two-year period, but each of us made that decision on our own. I was promoted to managing director, BearingPoint's partner equivalent, as promised. I also made an amazing selfless friend for life in Peter Wong.

And we were blessed with an incredible gift when Olivia was born the day after Christmas on December 26, 2002! We bought and moved into a new house in Davidson, a suburb of Charlotte, during this time to celebrate my promotion to managing director and to make a little more room for the new baby. In hindsight it is not a good idea to plan a move just before having a baby. It was a ridiculous decision as I remember Kelli having contractions at the closing when she was eight-months pregnant. Thankfully she didn't have the baby while signing mortgage documents! My issue with impatience was not always in my family's best interest.

In April of 2003, after eight months of stress and feeling like I was lost in the aftermath of the Arthur Andersen "fire sale," it got so bad I finally got on my knees, raised my hands, and cried out to God, *Lord, I will do whatever you want me to. Just please tell me what you want me to do.* But I added the qualifier: *If you want me to go to Africa, please convince my wife, Kelli, to go with me.*

That last part was silly looking back on it; I think God chuckled on that one. But we sometimes think a complete commitment to God might include this possibility. This was the first time in my life since I had accepted Jesus that I completely submitted my life, my family, and my career to him. My "burning platform" led me to this surrender.

But my spiritual walk before this time had its own twists and turns. I grew up in Somerdale, New Jersey, and can still vividly remember meeting God for the first time in what I fondly refer to as the "crazy church." My mom made us go. It was led by a Messianic Jew (a Jewish person who believes in Jesus) and held in a small elementary school. There was energetic music, dancing in the aisles, speaking in tongues, and attendance by people from many races and backgrounds. Whites, blacks, recovering drug addicts, and converted Jews. In a small classroom a kind woman who led Sunday School read to us from an illustrated children's Bible. I don't remember the story, but I remember feeling the love of God and looking back I see that this was my starting point. I believed in a loving God.

During my high school and college years I had what I would describe as a normal middle American experience. Life was smooth and fun, and I didn't think I needed God. When I read Scripture in college, during the few times I let a friend drag me to Bible study, I would argue or debate what we read. Looking back, I think I was just in my own world and thought I could figure things out on my own. I was still open to the idea that God and Jesus existed, but I didn't really need any help. "I got this" was the way I lived … until I didn't.

My first, big defining moment came after meeting Kelli, my future wife. It wasn't until I faced losing my relationship with her—because of my own stupidity in relying on alcoholic beverages more than I should—that I realized I needed to change what I was doing. I started attending church with her and being open and willing to learning about this God she and her family believed in. All I had to do was to be open—from that point God did the work of finding his way into my heart.

One night I cracked open a Bible my grandmother had given me. I opened it randomly and started reading. I would then jump to another part of the Bible, back and forth between the Old and New Testament. As I read Scripture the word that kept coming to me was *truth*. I agreed with what I was reading. God had given me new eyes to see; it was as if the words were coming off the page as I read. Four hours later I called my future wife to tell her I believed. In God. In Jesus. All of it. "What do I do next?" I asked.

The following day I walked the aisle at First Baptist Church in Kannapolis, North Carolina, and publicly accepted Jesus as my Savior. I would later be baptized. One year after that I would marry Kelli Lee, the love of my life, in that same church. It was a new beginning.

Are you open to a new beginning?

Think about this as you walk through this process with me. In my life I've experienced great joy and periods of terrible suffering. There have been points where I knew I was doing what God called me to do. There were also moments when I was lost, confused, and stuck in the wilderness without a map or compass. I promise you I will keep this story of what God has done in my life exactly as it happened, real. No sugar coating it, skipping over the mistakes I made or puffing myself up.

Through it all God has led me and held me, even when I didn't know he was there. I'm excited to share my experience and insights as a management consultant, entrepreneur, business person, and fired-up Jesus freak walking this road called Life. In those moments when I was lost it wasn't my strategic mind and hard work that got me out of trouble. In fact, that mindset—"I can figure this problem out"— is what has often gotten me into trouble. I needed to pray: "Not my will but your will be done, Lord."

My goal is to help you prepare to be found by a loving God and then to discover your God-given purpose and finally to learn how to find joy, even during the difficult times.

If you have made it this far, but are not ready for God to be an integral part of your life, that's okay. Continue on anyway. You will learn things about yourself that will be valuable. Being intentional and strategic about what you want in the future is a solid process, regardless of your faith journey. You can't hit a target you can't see.

Part Two

Finding My Purpose and Your Purpose

CHAPTER 3

Step One: Write Your Life Purpose Statement

What You Want to Be About

In the spring of 2003 God would lead me through a process that ended with a dramatic calling: "Mike, trust me. Do this North Highland thing."

Again I asked God for help. I even threw my hands up in frustration and said to God, *I'll do whatever you want me to do! Anything! Just show me.* That was an exhilarating and scary feeling. Did I mean that? Yes. So Kelli and I waited on the answer as I continued to work for BearingPoint, the firm that had acquired our consulting business from Arthur Andersen.

We waited . . . and waited . . . and waited.

As I've mentioned, patience is not one of my virtues. Over my life God keeps giving me lessons on being patient. My desire to quickly "fix" things and move on to the next item is intense, and it can get me in trouble when I get ahead of God or ahead of my wife and family.

Yet why was it taking so long? Now I know God was trying to teach me to come to him. I just didn't realize it.

In May of 2003 on a flight back from a conference in Las Vegas, of all places, I was reading *The Seven Habits of Highly Successful People*, and I was taking Stephen Covey up on his advice to write down my Personal Mission Statement (what I call a Life Purpose Statement) and write the obituary for my funeral, describing how I wanted my life to be remembered. To summarize the page-and-a-half of writing, my mission was to place my faith in Jesus and my family above my passions and interests in work. To stay true to this I realized it meant I had to stop traveling each week to allow me the time and flexibility to focus on what is most important.

My wife, Kelli, was taking the brunt of the new baby duties during my week-long business trips and also caring for a four and seven-year-old. She didn't ask, but I *knew* that something had to change! I began talking with North Highland again about that same position to start a Charlotte office. Providentially, the role was still open a year after I had been forced to turn it down.

At that moment I had a difficult decision to make. My partner Tim and I had been talking about different potential firms we might go to in the future or what we might do next. I felt that I needed to let him know what I was thinking about and I also had decided that I should invite him to talk to North Highland as well. I knew this meant he would be my boss again in Charlotte, rather than me having the opportunity to start and lead an office. But I knew it was the right thing to do.

He talked to North Highland and he told me they mutually agreed it was not a good fit for him, which I later learned was mostly about the salary being too low. He decided to pass and we agreed we would not discuss that opportunity again so it wouldn't create a conflict of interest.

Scott Evans, that persistent North Highland recruiter, kept on calling me. "You can do the same big-time consulting work with the brand-name clients you are used to, but do it only in Charlotte." This idea seemed like "having your cake and eating it too," so I rationalized it away for months and months as impractical. I reasoned again as I had before that if it worked, "Why wouldn't everyone do that?" Scott called me at least once per month for eight months.

A sick feeling in my stomach came early one morning, as it frequently did, as I packed my bags and prepared to leave Kelli, Alex, Cami, and Olivia for a week-long trip to Augusta, Georgia, so I decided to call North Highland back. They walked me through a verbal offer, which gave me something to think about during the three-hour drive.

I had driven to Augusta from Charlotte over fifty times and could almost do it on autopilot. The new job opportunity was exciting and frightening, all at the same time. I had just been promoted to managing director and a quick change seemed illogical. By the time I was close to Columbia, South Carolina, I had run through every possible scenario about what would happen if I stayed or resigned. I really wanted to be true to my newly written Life Purpose Statement, which I will share with you at the end of this chapter, but I was also responsible as the sole breadwinner in my family. I was leaning toward doing it, but was worried about the future.

Later I would remember the significance of that moment and the message God has for us in Jeremiah 29:11: "'For I know the plans I have for you,' declares the Lord, 'plans to prosper you and not to harm you, plans to give you hope and a future.'"[1]

About the time I reached Columbia, the halfway point, my cell phone rang. It was the lawyer Tim and I shared while pursing deals at Arthur Andersen. I hadn't heard from this lawyer in a long time. He said, "I'm calling you on behalf of my client (who was surprisingly my partner, Tim) to tell you I can't be your lawyer anymore and to tell you that at 2:30 today my client will be informing your new boss at BearingPoint that you are considering leaving the company."

I could not believe what I was hearing. The partner whom I'd worked with for seven years, whom I had invited to talk to North Highland, whom had talked to me about other opportunities to leave BearingPoint, was going to tell my new boss at BearingPoint! I didn't know what to say so I asked the lawyer if he could tell his client that I'd appreciate having until the next day before he did that.

As I hung up the phone a wave of worry and stress filled my whole body. I was gripping the steering wheel so tight I thought I might rip it off the column. We had a new house, a new baby, and now, once again, I was being faced with the prospect of my job being at risk. I was a bundle of nerves. My hand was being forced—which in hindsight was a blessing though that was far from how I felt at the time.

In this time of desperation, I called on the Lord. *Help me, please!*

I turned on my CD player and realized that a contemporary, Christian music CD by Mercy Me was there that had not been turned on in months. As I listened to the song "Word of God Speak," the lyrics and the music really spoke to me; they described being at a loss for words but feeling okay. Not needing anything but God's direction.

As I listened to the music and absorbed the lyrics the feeling that came next was something that I've never felt before or since. It started with the tingling on my hair and scalp; then the release and calm moved from my head to my neck, down my body to my legs, and out through my toes. It was as if the stress was being wrung out of me, as if God had a giant rolling pin he was moving down my body. All that was left was a beautiful, peaceful feeling. It was then that God spoke clearly to me. "Trust me," he said. "Do this North Highland thing."

It could not have been clearer what he was saying and that he had just spoken directly to me. I remembered that I had earlier told him, *Just tell me what you want me to do, Lord.* The feeling that had come over me propelled me from that point. *Yes, Lord,* was my reply, more through my actions than through a verbal response to him.

I immediately called the president of North Highland back and asked him to fax the offer to my hotel in Augusta. I let him know that if Morris Communications was okay with my decision I would be signing it and faxing it back to him in a few hours.

One hour later as I arrived at the hotel the fax was coming off the machine, an indication to continue ahead. And later, to my surprise the president of Morris Communications and my friend and client CFO Steve Stone were both very understanding and supportive. Will, the president of Morris Communications, said, "Mike, with three children I don't know how you've been doing it this long!"

How could they have such an unselfish view? I'm still amazed at this. Will is a Christian business leader so his unselfishness made sense to me, but it still gets me choked up to this day.

The next day on May 21, 2003, I began a journey at North Highland. Because I took the job when Alex was seven, I was home for much of his preteen-and-teen years. Cami was four and Olivia was one year old when I started this new chapter. I would not trade the experiences and the time at home with family for anything. Work was challenging, but we were trying to build a business that would allow people to do great consulting work and also stay committed at home with their families and in their communities.

During all these twists and turns, I wrote my Life Purpose Statement, which I will reveal to you as I invite you to formulate your own statement.

WRITING YOUR LIFE PURPOSE STATEMENT

This Life Purpose Statement is a written description of who you want to be when you grow up and what you want to be about.

Begin by asking yourself, What is the reason I was created? What kind of legacy do I wish to leave behind?

Using work techniques I've learned through over twenty-five years of strategic planning and consulting, we will write the story five, ten, and even fifteen years in the future.

Imagine that you are being interviewed by a reporter twenty years from now. Look back on your life from a future point. Think about what life looked like, what you did well, what people said about you. Give yourself permission to really dream big about what is possible.

Now come back to the present and begin to put your dreams into written reality. I will give you the notes that I made in April of 2003 when I was contemplating what I would do if I left BearingPoint. I will give you these thoughts before you write your own responses. Maybe they will help you discern your own.

Currently:
What do you do well? (I wrote, "I do complex consulting work, combining my background in strategic planning, accounting, and technology.")

Your Response

____

____

____

____

What do people say about you? (I wrote, "They say I work well with people, and that I'm persuasive in promoting ideas or solutions I believe are beneficial to my clients.")

Your Response

____

____

____

____

Five Years from Now:

What could you be doing then? (I wrote. "I am living out my faith more proactively and openly at work, and I'm integrating my faith, family, and work lives together.)

Your Response

____

____

____

____

What might people say about you? (I wrote, "People say that I place my faith and family as my top priorities, and that I live out my faith in Jesus by behaving and loving others like he does.")

Your Response

____

____

____

____

Ten Years from Now:
What could you be doing then? (I wrote, "I would be living a more balanced life and traveling less. I would be enjoying more freedom in my work and have a more entrepreneurial and fun working- environment.")

Your Response

____

____

____

____

What might people say about you? (I wrote, "People say I have incredible enthusiasm and energy for the work I'm doing and that my passion is contagious." Others might say, "I was able to give back to sustainable charities and possibly even start one to meet a need that God reveals to me.")

Your Response

____

____

____

____

Fifteen Years from Now:
What could you be doing then? (I wrote, "I could be starting or running my own company in a way that creates a strong business culture and set of values and makes a difference in the lives of others.)

Your Response

____

____

____

____

What might people say about you? (I wrote, "I could be taking risks and pursuing passions at work and through charities. I have prepared my children well for higher education and have raised them in a loving home in a way that was pleasing to God. We modeled the behavior we expected in our children and set a good example. We pointed our family, our friends, and our coworkers toward our Savior Jesus Christ.")

Your Response

____

____

____

____

Your Legacy

Next think about the legacy you wish to leave. . . .

My Example:

"I want to leave a legacy of love. Love for my wife, my children, my family and friends, and for the world. I want to help others who are hurting. I want to be remembered for always 'doing the right thing,' and I want to be known as someone who had a heart for God and for reaching people for Jesus. I want to be remembered as someone who integrated faith into work. I want to be remembered as someone who unselfishly gave to others."

Your Response

____

____

____

____

These exercises will help you identify the raw materials for your Life Purpose Statement. I also highly recommend engaging your spouse (or significant other) and your children/family in the process of writing your purpose statement and in defining success in your roles when you get to Step Two in Chapter Four.

In all our efforts to find God's purpose for our lives we need to be incredibly careful that we don't write our own purpose instead of writing what God reveals to be the purpose for our lives. Our intent needs to be: finding God's calling on our lives. When all else fails, we need to go to God's Word to find his purpose for our lives: to be conformed into the image of Jesus, which is very clear in Romans 8:28-29: "And we know that all things work together for good to those who love God, to those who are called according to His Purpose. For whom He foreknew, He also predestined to be conformed to the image of His Son, that He might be the firstborn among many brethren."

With this realization my goal is to live this way moment-by-moment, day-by-day for the rest of my days. When I get distracted or pulled by the world, when I make mistakes and sin, I will go back to this: abiding in and being obedient to all that Jesus is.

Alright! Now you are ready. I'm going to share the most current version of my Life Purpose Statement and then it is your turn to write the first draft of yours. Remember this is just a first draft. Take your time and do not get frustrated. Just focus on getting your rough ideas down and you can add to them later. This can take days, weeks, or months. Don't rush it. Take it to God in prayer. Lay it at the feet of Jesus and wait for him to inspire you. I pray, in Jesus name, that his inspiration will come to you in his perfect timing.

My Life Purpose Statement:
"To lead our family, business, and resources in a way that honors God and reflects the love, joy, and peace of Jesus and to passionately help others find an amazing, purpose-driven life."

Your Life Purpose Statement:

____

____

____

____

I've helped hundreds of clients and friends through the process of moving from one company or one job to another. This is the most powerful tool I've seen in helping people get clarity on their purpose and what they are looking for. Some people don't take the time to do this, even though it helps ensure that what they find fits their criteria for their priorities and their dreams. This is just a draft and can be a living, breathing document. Go to God in prayer for the next few weeks and months and continually ask him to show you his will for your life. Be patient and earnestly seek him and he will show you.

Now let us look at how we live our lives each day as we interact with those around us.

CHAPTER 4

Step Two: Define Success in Your Key Roles

Determine to Be Present

Back in 1996 when our first child Alex Lee was born, I had begun to examine my roles as a husband and a father. Having a child both expanded and rocked Kelli's and my world. Alex didn't sleep for eight months, forcing Kelli to quit her job. It turned out to be a blessing as our daughter Cami was born three years later, on May 28, 1999.

Despite the success at Arthur Andersen and a happy home life I had begun to feel the struggle and conflict between being a great husband and father and being "all-in" at work with the hours and the travel required of me. When Alex was about four years old and Cami was one, I had gone to a work retreat led by an outside facilitator. He had us do an exercise to think about the things that were most important to us and to identify an area we needed to improve upon. As I thought about this, I promised myself that I would try to be present when I was at home with my wife, my son, and my daughter.

The facilitator led us through an exercise where we wrote our commitment on a wooden karate board and then we each had to break it with our bare hand. Something shifted in me that day as I broke a board with my hand with the words "Be Present" on it. I was able to put my work aside once I got home and move it out of my mind to enable me to enjoy my wife and kids. I would envision me putting on my "Superman" cape—becoming super dad, super hubby. Sounds rather silly but during the early years the picture really helped me to focus on my family whenever I was with them. On December 26, 2002, Olivia Lee joined our family.

Take a moment to define the five-to-seven major roles you play in your life today and ones you'd like to add. In my original version it was Husband to Kelli; Father to Alex, Cami, and Olivia; Leader and Servant to the People I Work With; Advisor to My Clients; Teacher of the Bible and Musician (something I wanted to add to my life to bring me joy—playing the violin!).

Your major roles might look something like this: Husband or Wife, Father or Mother, Business Leader, Advisor, Christian, Single Person, Writer, Musician, Artist. Make this list your own and make it what you dream it could be. Focus on defining the top five-to-seven roles and don't stop until you have a passion for fulfilling those roles.

Now write a sentence or two about what success looks like in each of these roles – thinking about what your wife or husband, your children, your family, your employer, your coworkers, your clients might say—or maybe even ask them. Make sure to include your favorite hobbies (like my being a musician because of a desire to experiment and learn how to play the violin) and things that bring you joy.

My one-sentence Role Success Statements looked like this: Kelli would define success for me in my role as a husband as "You are present with me and the kids and are an active part of all of our lives." My daughter Cami would define success for me in my role as a father as "You sacrifice for us, you are present, and spend time with me, you listen to me, you are fun and funny, you lead us spiritually, you are a friend, and you provide structure." My employer would define success for me as an employee as "You are passionate about the work you do, you are instrumental in helping us grow, you work hard, and you are a good steward of the company's resources."

Role 1: ____________________

____

____

____

____

Role 2: ____________________

____

____

____

____

Role 3: ____________________

____

____

____

____

Role 4: ______________________________

____

____

____

____

Role 5: ______________________________

____

____

____

____

Role 6: ______________________________

____

____

____

____

Role 7: ______________________________

____

____

____

____

Fulfilling These Roles

After defining success in my key roles, I began to make changes in my life.

First as a Husband and Father.

As a husband and father, I was now able to give my family the gift of my time with my reduced travel. Olivia was still a small baby and Cami was four. Alex was a typical boy and at seven years old was quite a handful. He needed a lot of discipline at this early age and I was there to give it to him. It was an adjustment for Kelli and me in seemingly small things, like doing my fair share of the dishes and taking out the trash without being asked.

Still there were times when Kelli and I questioned our roles. The most memorable example was during a day in which nothing seemed to work right. My computer at work crashed after writing a proposal for twelve hours. I came home to enjoy the "benefits" of being local, which involved fighting traffic for forty-five minutes and arriving home a few minutes later than Kelli expected. During what I call "The Dark Winter," the post-partum period after Olivia was born, Kelli would hand me Olivia and say, "You're on!"

This particular night I pulled in the driveway and Kelli met me there, handing me baby Olivia. "Good luck," she said. "I'll see you later. . . . I'm going to bunko."

I was happy to give her some relief, but after a rough day at work I found it difficult to change gears and be Dad.

Still I rocked baby Olivia to sleep and then hurried Cami who was five and Alex who was eight to get ready for bed. Once there I shoehorned myself in-between them so I could read them a book.

It was then that Cami said, "Daddy, do you know how you get to heaven?"

This question, coming out of the blue, set me back. Alex and I were quiet for a second, contemplating our responses.

I spoke first, saying, "I think so, Cami, but why don't you tell me what you think?"

"Well, I'm going to build stairs and climb up to heaven." (Sounds like she was thinking of Jacob's ladder in the Bible or the song "Stairway to Heaven.")

Before I could respond, Alex, laying on my other side, scoffed, "Cami, that is stupid. You can't build stairs to heaven. That is *not* how you get there."

Being the peacemaker between older brother and little sister, I said, "Okay, Alex, why don't you share what you think. How do you get to heaven?"

Quickly he replied, "You have to be a good person, go to church, and do the right things."

I had listened to both intently, now it was my turn. "Cami and Alex those are great ideas. Now let me share with you how I think we get to heaven." Then I told them about God's grace, the story of how God sent his only Son Jesus to the earth to live and die among us, the perfect sacrificial lamb who willingly died on a cross so that our sins are forgiven.

"That forgiveness allows us to spend eternity in heaven with God and Jesus," I said. "All we must do is to let go and accept Jesus into our heart."

At the time I didn't want to push them further. I have always been very sure that deciding to accept Jesus is a very personal decision between that person and God. For now, I felt very content that I had explained the plan of salvation at their young ages. I gave them both a big kiss and hug and prayed with them.

What happened next was validation of my joining North Highland. After I turned the lights out and shut the door, I stood in the dark, quiet house and felt God whispering to me, *It's Wednesday.*

I stood there confused. I knew what I had heard but I didn't understand it. *So what?* I thought. *It's Wednesday.*

Then I felt him reply, *You were never here on Wednesday.* (Instead I was traveling with Arthur Andersen.) My loving God was showing me that my "hard" day was not what was important. If I hadn't been obedient to his calling, I would have missed the opportunity to have this conversation with my kids.

I stood in the hallway with tears of joy in my eyes. I was so thankful that, even though it was hard to start a North Highland office in Charlotte from scratch, I was truly given the opportunity to balance doing great and meaningful work and being present, leading and loving my young family.

After I defined success in my key roles, I also saw changes in my spiritual commitment, decisions I made in my role as a committed Christian.

As a Committed Christian

Because I wasn't traveling, Kelli and I both got more involved in our local church. Kelli taught the children in Sunday School, and I agreed to lead an adult Sunday School class. The required preparation for this class meant I was regularly in the Word of God, absorbing truth. Once I got a taste of God's Word I wanted more of it.

I kept a Bible on my desk at work and in the early days of starting up the business for North Highland in Charlotte I went to it frequently. During stressful times that had me anxious, I would open to the Psalms and read David's writings about peace and courage in times of trial. When I needed guidance from God, I would open to Proverbs and read from that book of wisdom, knowledge, and understanding.

Three months after Cami and Alex's conversation with me about heaven I also felt God direct me to share this benefit of local consulting work from the podium in front of eight hundred of my coworkers as a way of motivating our people as to why our work was so important. North Highland gave us the chance to have balance in an industry, not known for balance. (I told the story of my heaven conversation with them—without my sharing of the plan of salvation.)

Afterward I received an anonymous message written in the cover of a book. "Well done, Mike. There is a cloud of witnesses watching."

Another outcome of how my new calling changed my life was the integration of my faith into my work. After consulting with one client for a few years, I got up the courage to ask him if he would be interested in starting a men's Bible study in uptown Charlotte. I wish I'd done it sooner as it led to a weekly study that is still going on over fifteen years later. We meet at Ruth's Chris in uptown Charlotte and slowly and methodically read the Word, discuss what it means, and how it applies to our daily lives.

Still another result of my Christian commitment occurred in 2009 when our family started on an unexpected spiritual journey of investing in the Kingdom of God in San Jose, Costa Rica. During that summer our son, Alex, traveled with the family of his best friend Daniel Wyatt to explore ways they could help people in Latin America. They discovered that San Jose, Costa Rica, like most tier-one cities (top cities in population) had very poor and drug-infested areas with gangs and extreme crime.

They met Pastor William Padilla and his family through mutual friends and thus began an over ten-year effort to help serve the Kingdom of God in Costa Rica. Since that first trip our families and others have come alongside the Padilla's and their church, *Vuelo De Aguila*, which means "Flight of the Eagle." It all began on an abandoned soccer field in the inner city. Alex and Daniel were curious about why the barbed-wire, fenced-in grass field was empty while children were playing in the streets. The boys both spoke Spanish, and during a conversation with Pastor Padilla they learned that the field was owned by the city of San Jose and was available to rent. However, in the times when people could not afford to rent the field, the soccer field sat empty.

As the boys talked to Pastor Padilla about this, they explored the idea of pulling the teens off the streets, out of gangs, out of drugs, and onto the field by renting the field four hours per week. They called it "One by One" (*uno por uno*) www.onebyonecostarica.com, which was officially founded in 2010. The Lord had led me to fulfill my ten-year goal, which was "I was able to give back to sustainable charities and possibly even start one to meet a need that God reveals to me."

One of the teenage boys who is a great example of the life transformation that has taken place is Edgar. In 2010 Edgar showed up at the little One-by-One tent to register to play soccer. As he even now tells the story, he was high on drugs and was technically a leader of a gang at the time. He loved soccer though and wanted the chance to play. During those initial signups other gang members came and some even turned in weapons at the check-in. One boy brought an attack dog, which is a common means of personal protection in the area where they live. Even though most people think of the beautiful vacation spots of Costa Rica, it has a wide variety of socio-economic areas. We had decided to pitch our tent in the toughest part of San Jose, alongside our partner Pastor William Padilla.

Fast forward three years to March 20, 2013, and we are sitting on the concrete bleachers of a one- thousand-seat stadium, watching our top One-by-One boys' team play a successful local club team. Most of these players came from middle or upper-class families that could afford to have their children play year- round club soccer. We were all enjoying a beautiful sunny day in the center of San Jose, laughing and talking and watching the game, when we saw a player make a great move on the near sideline at about mid-field. He faked left with his head and body and then with lighting fast feet pushed the ball to the right with the outside of his right foot. The opposing player almost fell down he was so faked out. I then realized it was Edgar. Only Edgar had moves like that. Think of the feet equivalent of a pickpocket with incredibly fast hands.

Edgar pushed the ball in front of him eight yards and made long, fast strides down the right wing. I thought he was going to take it wide toward the far sideline and then cross the ball to the center, but instead he outran the defender who was struggling to catch up to him. Edgar still had the center sweeper to get past and the goal keeper. The ball took an uneven bounce on the not-so-perfect field as he sprinted toward the goal. With the opening he had created, Edgar launched a half volley before the sweeper could reach him. He hit the ball with the left edge of his left foot, which created a spin. The ball went from the right edge of the penalty box in a banana shape, penetrating the upper left corner of the goal perfectly between the crossbar and left post. It was a beautiful goal. One of those goals you have to scratch your head and say, "Did he do that on purpose?"

The crowd went crazy and we all jumped to our feet to show our pleasure. Edgar imitated what most top players do when they score: he ran the length of the goal line toward the near corner flag and then jogged over to midfield to receive his accolades from the crowd. That was when he stood straight at midfield facing us and raised his shirt up to show something written in Spanish—white lettering on a black t-shirt which was:

No yo sino la gracia de Dios en mi.

What does it say? we asked Edna Wyatt, the wife of my co-founder James Wyatt and our trusty Spanish translator. Edna turned around to us with a big smile and said,

Not me but the grace of God in me.

Tears welled up in my eyes as I realized not only how healthy and happy Edgar looked, but how he had been spiritually transformed.

What a moment this was. To be a part of God's plan and help make a difference like this in someone's life could not feel any better. I commented later to someone at work: "No matter what happens in the future, I will always have that one truly good thing that we did with God." If everything else falls apart we have that. Edgar would be baptized the next day and his place in heaven secured.

The night before we flew back to Charlotte, Edgar walked a mile to Pastor's house and asked him to bring this letter to us, which says it all:

From: Edgar To: Wyatt Family
Lee Family
Friends of project One by One

I hope you have received this letter, I wanted to thank you for all the sacrificie, trust and love that you have put 1x1 project in Costa Rica. For me it has been a great help in my life, because without that project really was not alive and I thank God so much for giving me a second chance and have sent angels with you! I have much appreciation, care and love to thank you for this great project I met God and he took care to change my life... I can never give back what you have given me much but I want to give this shirt, but do not see it as a simple shirt, see it symbolizing that you rescued a soul to the Lord...

Always remember that I will be praying for you and asking God to itself not the reward here on Earth, it is in heaven! I love you very much and remember that was in the soul and when the big teams playing football (that's my dream). I will remember...

God bless you always but always and love!

Farewell Cordially

Carefully:

Edgar Arteta #9
One by One Costa Rica.

Edgar spoke little English so we knew he had to look up most of these words in a Spanish/English dictionary. And he'd also sent us a gift: a t-shirt, like the one he'd worn at that soccer game. What a blessing! I've learned that when you give a blessing to someone, it is often returned in an unexpected way.

After the soccer events and church services in San Jose, we made our way in El Bus, the name we had all given to our rented, silly-looking, Partridge Family bus, to the Pacific Coast of Costa Rica and an all-inclusive resort called the *Riu*. This time it would be especially meaningful to take the whole Padilla family as they were having a tough year financially. Their church had been relocated to a temporary space and members' attendance and the Padilla's income was down. They were so grateful to have a chance to take a several day vacation at this beautiful resort.

At dinners we sometimes talked about the One-by-One program and the church so that we could determine how best to help and determine next steps for the year. Through our questioning we learned that the Padilla's had been without a car for a year. Their old one had broken down, and they didn't have the funds to get it fixed. With five children and four in school, this made things incredibly difficult on top of not being able to visit with church members easily. They were forced to use a taxi when necessary. The news of this broke my heart, and over the next few days in this beautiful place I could not get it out of my mind.

On the day before we were scheduled to leave, the Padilla, Wyatt, and Lee families enjoyed one more day on the beach and in the hotel pool. I was swimming around the pool, watching the adults talking and the children splashing and laughing, all of them speaking in Spanish. I was enjoying the moment when it hit me. . . . Or should I say God hit me. *Buy them a car,* the Holy Spirit whispered. I got a huge lump in my throat, realizing what this would mean to them. We had just gotten a bonus at work and we were able to do it. I swam over to Kelli and told her what I'd just felt. She immediately agreed, and we exchanged a glance of happiness and love. I then asked Edna Wyatt to ask the Padilla's and their family to swim over to the shallow end for a family meeting. Edna did not know what was going on, but she went along with it.

After everyone assembled in a circle in the shallow end of the pool, I said, "Edna, please tell the Padilla's that we would like to buy them a new car." As she repeated the news in Spanish Pastor Padilla dropped his head crying, his wife, Anais, screamed with excitement, and all of the children literally jumped for joy, piling on their overwhelmed parents. It was a beautiful experience for everyone involved. It meant so much to us to be able to do this for this family we had grown to love. It also enabled them and the church to get back on their feet that year. It was a signal of brighter days ahead for the Padilla's and for their church.

The Wyatt family and many generous donors have been the ones who have made all this work in San Jose possible. I thank them for the gift of their time and treasure to help serve others. Daniel and Alex played the leadership role in One by One in the first few years before they headed off to college. Since then, it has been amazing to watch the Wyatt's and our other children continue this role in the program, raising money and leading the annual visits. Ben Wyatt, Amelia Wyatt, Cami Lee, and Olivia Lee have all stepped up to play successive roles of leadership. It has been wonderful to have One by One be a dual family affair.

I am glad that I took time to consider success in my roles. Now it's your turn.

Fulfilling Your Roles

Think about the roles that you mentioned earlier and the success that you desired in those roles. How can you make some definite plans to fulfill those roles even more successfully?

List those roles here and then note any specific future plans you might want to take.

____

____

____

____

No matter what, I want to encourage you, whether you are young or old, to identify something you can do to care for others in another country or for the people right in front of you. We don't have to wait until "retirement" or until we have enough money to do something. It's amazing what a difference a small amount of money can make. Instead use what you have right now. Use your time, your talents, and yes, some of your financial resources to get started and stay with it. Use what you have, don't wait. Do it with a heart for others, but I promise you, and more importantly God promises you, it will bless your life and that of your family in multiples.

More than a thousand teens and adults came to believe in Jesus through the soccer program and the church over the nine-year period after the boys and Pastor Padilla got the idea for One-by-One. We have loved them so much, and they have returned the love ten times ten. Nothing can explain the beautiful things that have happened, except an incredible, loving God—the God described in the Bible who performs miracles today as he did two thousand years ago.

CHAPTER 5

Step Three: Find a Job That Fits Your Calling

Consider Your Gifts, Your Experiences, and Your Passion

By 2011 our growth rate at North Highland slowed to the teens as the Big Four accounting firms all reentered the consulting market, hiring and deploying hundreds of thousands of consultants. It was ridiculous, in my opinion, that the government allowed the Big Four to reenter consulting when the conflict of interests between a firm having audit and consulting had been identified as a contributor to the downfall of Enron. These firms all had sold off or shrunk their consulting units until their non-competes ran out and/or the economy improved to the point they could convince the regulators they had control over the conflicts.

With the slowed, but still profitable, growth, it was "all hands-on deck" to identify strategies to compete with the bigger firms. I worked with Paramjit Uppal, the founder of the United Kingdom consulting business we had acquired, to facilitate a strategic-planning exercise, which called for an investment in building expertise areas to complement our relationships with the companies we served. It was during this period of laying out a new game plan that our CEO, Dan Reardon, came to Charlotte. This is the same man who had made me the offer to join the company back in 2003. We were getting ready to sell our house in Davidson and move somewhere else in the community. I decided to tell him as I didn't want him to think I was leaving if he heard about the house being on the market.

"Why don't you move to Atlanta?" he asked that day in March. "You are the logical succession candidate over the next couple of years." I remember it was like time stood still. I had always been told a move to Atlanta was not needed, even to be considered for CEO, but now the game was changing. I asked him for a month to think about it, pray about it, and talk it over with my wife and family.

I wrestled spiritually with the decision for about four weeks from the time Dan asked me to move. *Lord, what do you want us to do?* I begged. I prayed several times daily and asked God to help me make the right decision. Although I was open to God's direction I was also feeling impatient. The fact that our lives were completely up in the air was a very stressful situation.

I decided to book a room at the Cove, the Billy Graham Conference Center in the mountains of North Carolina, to create alone time to think and pray and seek God's direction. My plan was to spend two full days with nothing but a Bible and nature.

I was going to "go up on the mountain" and obtain the answer from God.

God had other plans.

The Saturday before my trip to the mountain, I awoke from a very restless sleep and a dream about my work. I got up without waking Kelli and went into my closet with a to-do list in my head. Half asleep I grabbed a pen from the shelf there and began jotting down the list of to-dos that had come to me in my dream. Considering moving and working with North Highland at the same time was stressful; now I was even working in my sleep!

As I finished the list of five things I needed to take care of and lifted the pen from the page I felt God speaking to me. *Just go,* he said. I felt amazing relief to get this clear direction even though it was not the answer I knew Kelli would want. We had never gone wrong following God's calling and I immediately shifted to "make-it-happen mode."

I woke Kelli up and delivered the mixed news that we had our answer, which was good but also bad since it meant we were off to Atlanta. She accepted the news well and trusted my calling as she always had, yet I could tell she was not convinced. Kelli, also a very analytical person who thinks through all the bad things that can happen in any given situation, needed more. She needed her own calling. This was too big a decision to go on blind faith. Was it really a calling? Kelli wondered.

Being the patient guy that I am, insert sarcasm here, I immediately cancelled my trip to the Cove and decided to go to Atlanta on Sunday and Monday to look at houses and schools. I was in implementation mode. Friends had told me that it was critical to get started on schools, because the deadline for applications was coming up in just two weeks.

I began the process by talking with a few trusted colleagues about what we were looking for in schools, neighborhoods, commute time, and churches. Then I zeroed in on an area north of Atlanta that had two highly recommended private Christian schools, great neighborhoods, proximity to North Point, our favorite church to attend when visiting Atlanta, and a commute that was no longer than the one I had from Davidson. Cami had off from school, so she accompanied me on the trip. We looked at about ten houses and drove by the schools. The area was busy, but had pretty neighborhoods nestled all along the Chattahoochee River, which spills out of Lake Lanier to the north and meanders all across the north section of the Atlanta area on its way to where it empties into the Gulf of Mexico via the panhandle of Florida. For some reason the feeling of living "way down yonder on the Chattahoochee" appealed to me.

Looking back on it the process was like a blur. I made plans to take Kelli and the kids as well as Kelli's parents Gene (whom we call Paw, Paw) and Irene (whom we call Nanny) with us to house hunt the following weekend. I put everyone up in the Marriot Extended Stay and we spent the whole weekend looking at schools and houses. For parts of the day we split up when the girls were tested as part of their application to school.

After Kelli refused all the houses Cami and I had found, she and our agent ventured out on their own. Around lunchtime on Saturday Kelli called and said, "Mike, I found something really interesting. I've never wanted to live in a house that someone else has lived in, but this one is different. It is beautiful. My mom agrees."

We met for lunch, and she quickly talked me through why she didn't like the other homes she'd seen so far. With a dampened enthusiasm she said, "This one might work." She slipped me a picture of the home and told me she had never seen such quality construction. It was more than we were looking to spend, but I didn't want to squash the slight enthusiasm she was showing. After all, if I was asking her to move away from her parents for my job, I figured I needed to make sure she was happy. Having been married almost twenty years I am a subscriber to the theory "If Mamma ain't happy, ain't nobody happy!" The flaw in my reasoning might have been thinking I could make Mamma happy with a house.

The next day we went to the home. It was situated in North Atlanta where Roswell meets Alpharetta, right on the banks of the Chattahoochee River. The neighborhood was named Ellard after the family that had owned this large swath of land for over a century. From the highest point in the neighborhood you could see Holcombe Bridge, the main road outside of the neighborhood, which marked the original spot where people had forded the river since the late eighteenth century. The site around that section of the river is an historic one, having been used as a makeshift hospital during the Civil War.

As the whole family pulled into the Ellard Gate, Alex sang "We will be living in a gated *communiteh-ee-eh-ee-eh- aaaa.*" We all laughed and would remember that silly song for years. When we had first started looking in Davidson years before, Alex had come up with the idea of living in a gated community, because he was anxious about safety after neighborhood break-ins. I'd let him watch too many episodes of "Cops" and "Life in the ER" when he was little. He was always waiting for the axe to fall.

I was immediately captured by the Charleston feel of the homes and streets. It was like a little oasis in the midst of a bustling tier-one city. You could walk on the brick sidewalks and in the parks without worrying about the traffic. I felt relaxed as we made our way past the main park in the center of the neighborhood. We turned left and were quickly in front of the house.

I walked in and was immediately excited as I looked right and gazed upon the most amazing study I'd ever seen. The wall was lined with custom-made, book shelves and the walls and ceiling were covered with wood paneling that had been hand carved and set in place with amazing workmanship. Given my love for American history, family history, and artifacts, I was immediately drawn to this home that had a place for my book and history collection. As I emerged from the study I noticed Kelli's Dad sitting on the bench in the entryway. "What do you think Paw Paw? I asked.

"That's a lot of space to keep clean."

"Yeah," I replied as I made my way upstairs to meet Kelli and her mom.

He was right, for sure, but it was also not like him to look at the negative side of anything. It had been about eight months since Gene's stomach started hurting terribly and he couldn't sleep well at night. He had plopped down on the bench in the foyer where he stayed the whole time we looked at the house.

Next, I walked downstairs and into the kitchen area. Immediately I knew why Kelli liked this house. The kitchen was amazing with nice appliances, beautiful custom cabinetry, and granite countertops. Even though it was so well done, it did not seem pretentious. We would later look back on the house with fondness. There was a comfortable, family feeling to the place.

After looking at over twenty homes Kelli had found something she could get excited about so we thought about making an offer as we returned home to Charlotte on Sunday. That night as Kelli and I went to bed, we talked about the whole weekend.

"I'm still not sure we should move, Mike. This is a hard decision. I know you've gotten your calling from God, but I haven't yet. . . . I'm just not there yet. I think this is a good move for your job, and if we are going to do it, we should probably do it now so Cami wouldn't have to switch in high school. This is such a big decision; I just really need a sign from God that we are doing the right thing."

"Let's just keep praying for guidance, and if you need a sign, I pray that God will give you one. It has made all the difference for me to know that even though it is difficult, and not what I want, I am following God's plan and being obedient to his will," I said.

Kelli would later tell me that she really wanted that house. She wasn't sure we would find anything better. As she lay there, trying to go to sleep, she asked God for the sign she needed. *Lord, if you want us to go to Atlanta, make the final house price include the numbers 1335, in that specific order.* She just picked what she thought was a random number between the owner's list price and what we had hoped to pay. She kept this to herself because she felt guilty about being so fixated on that house.

The next day I was at work when my agent called. The owners of the house had been thrown off by our low offer, but because they were in a hurry to move to Florida, they made what they felt was a really appealing counteroffer, as low as they would go.

"They countered with what I think is a good offer, Mike," our agent, Carol, said.

"*Hmmm,*" I said as I did some mental calculations. It was at the upper limit of what I wanted to spend, for sure, but I really needed to have Kelli and the kids on board with the move.

"Let me give Kelli a call, but I think we might be able to make that work." I hung up the phone and called Kelli. "Hey, babe, we got a counteroffer and I think it is a pretty good one."

"What is it?"

I told her the number and it included the numbers 1, 3, 3, and 5, which seemed very random to me.

For about ten seconds I couldn't hear anything on the other end of the line; I looked at my phone to make sure it was still connected as I asked, "Kelli, are you there?"

It was then that I could hear Kelli sobbing.

"Are you okay, Kelli?"

"Yesss, Mike, I guess we are moving to Atlanta."

"What do you mean, Kelli?"

"The numbers 1, 3, 3, and 5 are the exact numbers I prayed over last night and in that specific order. I asked God to show me a sign and he did."

Kelli had pulled over to the side of the road and cried with her head in her hands. She knew that God had given her what she asked for and now she was going to have to say goodbye to North Carolina and head off to the big city of Atlanta.

Now we both let go and accepted the move. We had a lot of work ahead of us, but we were in forward motion and that felt good. Our wagon wasn't stuck anymore so we started to make our way down that Great Wagon Road to a point further south than anyone in our family line had gone before.

After this month of thinking and praying and discussing the whole family thought it was the right thing to do. Even my son, Alex, who was going into his senior year of high school, thought it was a great move. Would it be? Would it be a peak or was there a deep valley on the other side? We decided to look at it as an adventure, and we all took the plunge together.

Our first week in Atlanta, in June of 2013, the girls were staying with me at a resort north of Atlanta called Lake Lanier Island while Kelli and Alex stayed back in North Carolina to oversee the moving out of the house in Davidson. During my day off we went to an old waterpark and rode on an aging concrete waterslide. I ignored the weight limit on this old waterslide—"Caution 230-pound weight limit." I thought, *I'm pretty close to that.*

Big mistake.

My daughters and the slide operator watched in horror from the top of the slide as I took flight – in slow motion—lifting off from the concrete flume and crashing back hard onto it ten yards below. Maybe my "extra cushion" softened the blow.

Thankfully I survived this incident, but I guess I won't blow off the weight limit the next time. (I must have been about 240 pounds at the time.) Some actions in life require more precise standards, it seems. I guess that weight-limit warning was more than a suggestion!

We made a hard landing into Atlanta on the slide and in life – the bumps and bruises I received as I flew into the air and crashed head long into concrete was foreshadowing that this would not be an easy journey. I had heard of pastors being called into the ministry by God but had never heard of someone being called into a business or secular occupation. We had had an amazing run at North Highland, growing an average of thirty percent per year for more than ten years. But with the Big Four accounting firms rebuilding their consulting businesses we had leveled out at approximately $400 million in revenue. Even though we were consistently profitable there was pressure to get the growth rate high again and that meant changes were afoot at the company.

Looking back on the situation, it didn't take long for things to start going sideways. In the fog of a move with three kids and a big job at work I wasn't seeing clearly. Just ten days after my fall off the water slide, my eyes were focused on the stacks of packing boxes in front of me at our new Atlanta home. As we unpacked the moving truck I received a call from the CEO, Dan Reardon. "Hey Mike, how is the move going?"

"Pretty well," I said, as I stood in our new kitchen with boxes piled over my head. I'd been unpacking for hours and had barely moved the pile an inch down from the ceiling.

"I need you to come out of your day-to-day role of leading the operations of our business (as president) so that you can focus on building the new areas of expertise in our strategy."

I was too overwhelmed with piles of packing boxes, the move, and the impact on my family to fully comprehend what was happening so I simply said, "Sure, Dan, I'll see you on Monday."

I remember feeling a twinge of doubt about what this meant, but I pushed those bad thoughts away and took the man at face value. Surely, he couldn't be pushing me out of my president role and CEO succession when he had just asked me to move. I'd worked for the company for eleven years, and we'd experienced incredible growth and stability.

We had gone from two employees in Charlotte to over one hundred and fifty and opened new offices in the United States, eventually covering most tier-one U.S. cities in twenty-three offices. We had acquired a company in the United Kingdom, which now was going well, and established partnerships in many European countries and several in Asia.

North Highland had experienced an average growth rate of 30 percent and had been consistently profitable from 2003 to 2013. It was a great ten-year run, and we ended up ranked in the top 4 Places to Work in the World in *Consulting Magazine* for seven years straight—ranked by the responses of our people! I hadn't changed during my trip down Interstate 85 from Davidson. What had changed?

On Monday morning Dan and I got together to iron out what he was looking for. Because I had created the expertise development strategy with the founder of our U.K. operations, Paramjit Uppal, I was up to speed on what would be required to be successful. For us to compete with the Big Four firms and serve the biggest companies in the United States and the United Kingdom, we needed to invest in building deeper, subject-matter expertise in our client's industries and in building deeper, functional expertise in marketing, finance, and information technology. I had written the playbook with Paramjit, and now I was being asked to come out of my day job, running the company, to focus on this new strategy. I was keeping the president title, but the overall influence of my role was being diminished.

I was in denial for a while. I could not comprehend how things changed so quickly upon my arrival. Yet I was so absorbed with helping my family acclimate to a new city, new schools, and leaving their friends behind that I guess I compartmentalized this. I mentally decided to keep doing my best at the new strategy work as I knew it was critical to the company's future sustainability. Yet in the back of my mind I was thinking, How could this be happening?

I was stressed at work and my family was stressed with the move. We were being pressed and tested – it was another burning platform. The fire was getting hotter and I knew something was going to need to change.

By December of 2013, six months into our relocation to Atlanta, I realized that I was in a career situation that was not sustainable. I was fighting the good fight at work but was increasingly getting nowhere. Something had to give. There had to be a change, not just for the company but for me and my family.

In January of 2014 I recorded in my journal that I was losing my passion for consulting. I didn't enjoy it anymore. Was the problem my profession or my environment?

This was a moment when I needed to make sure that I was working in a job that fit my calling. Because I had been at North Highland for more than a decade of growth, had hired so many people that worked there, and had poured so many hours into it as a startup, it was hard to mentally think about letting go or walking away now that we were getting to mid-size and sustainable profitability. It felt like it was a part of me. I had promoted the mission and business model of having a great consulting career and raising a family at the same time and was a strong protector of the culture and values we espoused. So much of supposedly "the best years" of my working life had been poured into this company.

My job at this time was to look again for a job that fit my calling. You might be just starting to work or you might be considering another job, because of the environment you are in or because you might not be where your gifts and experiences are being utilized.

This is the moment to take a talents and life-experiences inventory and also an inventory of your spiritual gifts. Let's begin with your talents and life experiences. I will show you how I go through this process and then you can note your own talents and life experiences.

Talents and Life Experiences Inventory

My Talents and Life Experiences	Your Talents and Life Experiences
My Talents Management consulting Strategic thinking Analysis and problem solving Speaking and writing Business leadership	**Your Talents**
My Life Experiences Accounting and profit and loss management Entrepreneurship and business growth Experience dealing with pride and specifically making accomplishments an idol (More about that in Chapter 9.) Helping people deal with addiction to alcohol Helping people deal with anxiety and depression	**Your Life Experiences**

Now consider your spiritual gifts.

Spiritual Gifts Inventory

Work through the graph on th next page, rating your gifts as either primary (P) or secondary (S). There you will see a description of the gift and then you can do your evaluation of your own gifts beside it. I will work through this graph with you as you do so. This list comes from the Bible: Romans, Chapter 12 and 1 Corinthians 12.

Gift	Description	List Primary (P), Secondary (S) or Not Applicable (NA)
Teaching	Discovers and validates truth and shares it.	Mine – (S) Yours –
Exhortation	Encourages and motivates people to grow spiritually through counseling, teaching, preaching, and mentoring others.	Mine – (P) Yours -
Giving	Has passion for sharing resources.	Mine – (S) Yours –
Leadership, Organization, and Administration	Leads an organization and carries out projects.	Mine – (P) Yours –
Mercy	Demonstrates God's love by responding to others hurt.	Mine – (S) Yours –
Healing	Able to bring physical, emotional, or spiritual healing.	Mine – NA Yours
Serving	Has passion and willingness to serve others.	Mine – NA Yours –
Discerning of Spirits	Has capacity to discern the source of spiritual manifestation, whether it is a good or evil spirit.	Mine – NA Yours -

Once you have recorded your talents and experiences and your spiritual gifts, you are ready to look over the charts above and think about the job that might be worthwhile for you. What avenue might the Lord want you to take? How can God use your unique gifts and talents and your life experiences to bring him glory?

As I thought about this I noted my spiritual gift of exhortation and my experiences with growing businesses.

Note some of your own ideas here:

____

____

____

____

My decisions at this time were gradual, because of my dedication to my company, my colleagues, and my clients, yet slowly but surely, I pulled back out my Life Purpose Statement and stared at it: the words reflected my desire to focus on my faith, my family, and on building, leading, and growing things. My mind was foggy as I read it.

You will want to compare the thoughts above with your Life Purpose Statement. I have said that this is a living, breathing document.

Record your Life Purpose Statement here:

____

____

____

____

Then evaluate it as you look through your answers in the Talents and Life Experiences graph and the Spiritual Gifts Inventory.

Do you need to make any changes? If so, record your new Life Purpose Statement here:

____

____

____

____

Now you are ready to develop the profile of a job that fits your calling. The profile I wrote in 2014 was "With my spiritual gifts of exhortation and leadership/organization and my experiences with growing businesses and my renewed passion for consulting I identify my job profile as: a growth-oriented, consulting business leader."

Now write your own profile here:

____

____

____

____

As I went through this process, way off in the distance, through the fog, I could see the faint light of a lighthouse—a beacon guiding me through the storm to the safety of a new port. This was not the path I would have chosen, but it was the one God was allowing me to go through. He was with me, in the boat, and I would need him so badly.

CHAPTER 6

Step Four: Be Aware of God's Guidance

His Direction Can Come in Unexpected Ways

While the career situation slipped into discontent, our family was experiencing turmoil as well. My daughter Cami had a serious concussion from falling down a flight of concrete steps at school. Both our girls were very stressed at school, Kelli had a cancer scare, and Olivia was struggling with anxiety. Other than that, everything was fine!

On top of that, Kelli's parents Gene (Paw Paw) and Irene (Nanny) who were supposed to move with us—we had a furnished basement ready for them—now showed no interest in moving to Atlanta. Nothing about "our plan" was working.

Six months after our move to Atlanta, my son, Alex, decided he wanted to go back and finish high school in North Carolina. We knew Alex would graduate in May and hopefully go on to college, but we did not know whether he should stay in his current school in Atlanta or pull him out and send him back to his old school in North Carolina. We were struggling mightily with the choice. We didn't want to do anything rash after all that we had been through. It was a tough and exhausting week as I was sick and dealing with the stress. We prayed hard from morning to sundown for several days for God's guidance on whether Alex should stay in Atlanta or return to North Carolina, finish high school that May, and go on to college.

On Thursday morning, January 9, 2014, Kelli prayed again, but this time for discernment rather than a specific answer. During her time with God she heard him speak saying, *You need to focus on the right environment for Alex.* Kelli doesn't often tell me she has a clear message from God but she was sure this time. He gave her two words— *right environment.* We had peace with the message, but we still didn't know the solution—where is the right environment?

Given all that we'd been through God knew that we needed strong leading. We needed a two-by-four to the head, not whispers. And that's what happened on Friday, January 10, when we experienced a series of incredible events. Over the ensuing eight hours God seemed to put some special people in our path to help guide us.

The first of these was Durwood Snead whom I met for coffee that Friday morning. A few weeks earlier I'd set up a meeting with him through a mutual friend at work. He is the head of Global Missions at North Point Church, the church we had attended since moving to Atlanta.

Near the end of our meeting, we were both looking at our watches as I needed to get home to help Kelli and Alex with college applications and Durwood needed to get to his next meeting at North Point. The time had flown by and we had really connected. Durwood was a former business guy like me and now served full time in the ministry. I had prayed before our meeting that we would talk about all the things God intended.

Even though it would now make him late, Durwood looked me in the eyes, paused for a moment, and then he said—out of the blue—"How is your son doing, Mike?" The look in his eyes was peaceful and caring and I knew where this question was coming from. God prompted him to ask me. Durwood went on to tell me that his son had gone to the same high school that Alex was in and that he had to remove him for the same reasons we were now worrying about for Alex—it was not a good environment! We said goodbye, and as I drove back home I knew that this was God gently nudging me toward getting Alex out of this school. Selfishly I didn't want to see him go, but I was starting to think it might be the wise choice.

When I got home I shared the information with Kelli. She reiterated what God had placed on her heart – *the right environment.* We decided to take Alex to lunch to discuss his options at our favorite sushi restaurant Sushi Uchi, which was located in front of our neighborhood.

At what seemed like our weakest moment at an ordinary restaurant something extraordinary happened.

Kelli, Alex, and I sat down at our usual table for lunch, thinking we would talk about the situation and try to figure out our next move. We had been praying so hard for the last two days, dropping to our knees more than a few times to seek guidance. We were the only people in the place, except for a woman and her young son seated next to us. Early in our lunch I had noticed them talking about her son doing some public speaking to encourage people to give to an organization they had created called Aidan Cares, a ministry to inspire people to have giving hearts. I noticed the boy's backpack, which was colorful and looked like something a child much younger would carry.

The Holy Spirit whispered to me, *You need to talk with them.* I thought it awkward to just interrupt their lunch and introduce myself, so I waited. I was also trying to stay present with Alex and Kelli as we discussed our impending decisions. Soon the woman and her son finished their lunch, got up, and moved toward the door while talking with our favorite waitress Winny. I thought I'd lost my chance to talk to them. It is not often I get that nudge from the Holy Spirit, so I felt bad that I'd not made an effort. They stopped at the door and I watched the boy pull out a harmonica and put it to his lips. He started playing the blues for Winny. *How odd a scenario*, I thought as he played his harmonica. His mother looked over my way and we caught each other's eye.

I said, "Hello."

She walked right over and sat down next to me on the booth; her son also joined us. "Hello," the woman said, "my name is Toren. God sent me over to talk to you."

"That is funny because I was getting the same message to talk to you," I replied.

Toren looked over to Kelli and Alex and introduced herself and Aidan, her son, to them. Then she asked, "So what is going on with this guy?"

"Well, we are really struggling with whether to keep him here in school somewhere or send him back home to North Carolina to finish out his senior year," Kelli explained.

"What I am getting from God is that you need to urgently get him out of the situation he is in and send him back to North Carolina. He needs to be there in the right environment," Toren said.

Kelli and I looked at each other in disbelief. A random lady walks up to us at Sushi Uchi, tells us to send him back, and uses the same exact words God had given Kelli just hours before – *the right environment.*

That was all Kelli and I needed to know that Toren and Aidan might have been sent to us by our Heavenly Father. From the expression on Alex's face I could tell he was still skeptical. Perhaps he thought they had listened to our conversation.

It was then that Aidan asked Alex, "How are you doing?"

Alex looked at him kind of skeptically and answered, "Pretty good."

Aidan turned toward Alex. "God has big plans for you, Alex. He wants you to be way up here." He motioned with his hand above his head. "Right now, you are operating down here," and he placed his hand out in front of his waist. It was almost comical to see this twelve-year-old whom we had just met ministering and challenging our seventeen-year-old son. It left Alex with a look on his face like, "Who do you think you are?"

A lot was said in that twenty-minute encounter but here are the highlights of what Toren predicted as we were talking, all of which ended up coming true over the next three years:

- We needed to get Alex back to North Carolina. Don't wait on a solid plan just send him. Toren shared that when God parted the Red Sea to save his people he required Moses to take action, first by waving his arms to command the sea to part.

- In twelve-to-eighteen months something *really* big was going to happen or change. This was the same timeframe Pastor Padilla would give me during our trip in the upcoming spring. It sounded exciting.
- I was instructed to read Job, as if preparing me for what was ahead. I knew this meant tough times, which absolutely came true. I prayed, *Lord, please just don't let the devil take my wife or children.*
- We needed to "Circle the Wagons"—stick together geographically and/or spiritually. This was to prepare us for the assault that was going to come at us.
- Alex was like a biscuit that is not yet done in the middle. He had tremendous potential and would do great things for God, but he was not fully matured.

Toren asked all three of us for our cell phone numbers so she could stay in touch. As we walked out of the restaurant, we were in a bit of a shock from information overload. That kind of thing doesn't happen to you every day. And it does seem very strange. We might have met someone with an apparent prophetic gift, but we were trying to absorb it. Alex and I drove home together, and Kelli drove her car separately. As I pulled away Alex expressed doubts, and I think the entire encounter seemed weird to him.

What we didn't know at the time was how unusual Aidan Anderson was and the difference he has made in the lives of others. The ministry Aidan Cares was founded by this young boy after he received eighty dollars in tips for playing his harmonica at a restaurant. He immediately decided to give what seemed like a fortune to that seven-year-old boy to a charity to fight parasites for children in Africa.

Since then Aidan has spoken throughout our country and on TEDx Talks, encouraging parents and adults to model giving to the children in their lives. He was awarded the Daily Point of Life Award, which is given to individuals who spark change and improve the world, for these inspiring talks.

Yet another encounter, which seemed to verify the authenticity of what God was trying to tell us, occurred immediately after we left the sushi restaurant when Kelli pulled into our Ellard neighborhood gate, just forty yards from the restaurant.

We had been in Atlanta for six months by then and passed through the gate to our neighborhood hundreds of times. The exchange with the man who worked at the gate during the daytime was always the same. "Hello, how are you?" Kelli would say, and he would reply "Fine, how are you?"

For six months the exchange was nothing more than "Hello's" and never any deeper. However, on this day, when Solomon said, "Hello, how are you?"

Kelli replied, "Not so great, we are really struggling with what to do with Alex."

"What do you mean?" the guard gate replied.

"Well, we are struggling with whether Alex should stay in his school here or go back to North Carolina to finish high school."

Without hesitation Solomon said, "I've been watching Alex come and go since he got here, and he does not look content or happy. He needs to go."

Kelli was amazed by the conviction that Solomon had in his voice, which occurred minutes after we had received the urgent warning from our new friend Toren. Four days later, after we had decided to re-enroll Alex in Cannon School in North Carolina, we received the following email from Solomon:

January 14, 2014
Mrs. Kelli
Mr. Michael

I am happy to hear the good news this morning. And I feel very much honored to have me share with you such an important matter very close to your heart.

I always wanted to say something, and it didn't take me much to engage in the discussion with Mrs. Kelli when the subject was slightly mentioned. As a father of four children, I do understand and fully identify with the changing behaviors of children at each stage of their growth. We parents take some things for granted. But every sign in the development of children is as important as any other.

From my brief discussion with Mrs. Kelli the other day, I can feel how you made his interest the center of your life here. Rightly so. And it paid off. And amazingly the answer came in the form of a biblical intervention worthy of a book. And also, that says a lot about your standing in the face of God.

Congratulations.
Solomon at the Gate
Solomon Gizaw

During a return trip to Atlanta in May of 2014, I stopped at the gate to talk with Solomon. We shared hellos, and then I let him know Alex was doing well and adjusting to life in North

Carolina; he had already received acceptance letters from three colleges.

I wanted to learn more about Solomon, because Kelli had mentioned to me that he had been an Ethiopian judge. "Kelli told me you are from Ethiopia and that you had been a judge at one time," I said.

"That is correct," Solomon replied. "I went to law school and became a lawyer and worked for the government, and at one time had my own private practice and was a lawyer."

"How did you end up here, Solomon?" I asked.

"Well, I really wanted a better life for my four children and hoped to send them to America to get a good education. We entered the visa lottery for the U.S. and my wife was granted a visa. I thought about sending her here with the children without me, but had friends who were already here and advised that I wait until we all could come. I was also hesitant to give up my law practice. Eventually though I decided to leave."

Solomon then got a big smile on his face and said, "My children have been very successful. Three of them have masters degrees and are doing well, and the fourth will graduate from college soon."

A car pulled in behind me, cutting our conversation short. "Have a great day, Solomon," I said. "You too, Mr. Mike."

What a wonderful love this father had for his children. Solomon sacrificed everything for his family. He is a pioneer, risking everything he knows to give his children a better chance in life. God used Solomon, a former Ethiopian judge, to guide us on our correct path.

God speaks in so many ways, if we could only listen. If we could only focus our attention and understand that every aspect of our lives is his blessing. Most times his presence is not as obvious, but many of us believe that there are no co-incidences in life.

For the next few months, I traveled back and forth from Davidson to Atlanta, caring for my family and doing my absolute best to keep my work moving forward. In my toughest moments I would remember Kelli's advice to "Work each day as if you are working for the Lord."

It is easy to work hard and do great work when things are going well and when we know we are fulfilling God's purpose for our life. But it is so hard to show up and do good work when we don't feel treated well, and we are confused about where we are heading. In those moments we must remember that everything we do is a testimony about us and about our Jesus, about our God. When all else fails, no matter what is going on, we must remember that we represent him.

I greatly admire people who can show up and "Be his light" in the world in tough jobs, with unforgiving bosses and bad situations. We honor God by doing the right things and serving others when no one is looking. It's not the famous who deserve admiration. It is those who quietly "Take up their cross" and follow him daily, no matter their circumstances. Look for the people with a smile on their faces who don't seem to be in situations where they should have one. And remember to be a blessing to one of these people who deserve it.

CHAPTER 7

Step Five: Analyze Where You Are

Recalculate Your Priorities

Looking back on it, Alex's move back to Charlotte was like the advance force in a military operation. His location was a blessing as it was critical in preparation for what would happen next. That occurred on February 2, 2014 when my wife's father died just two weeks after getting Alex into his apartment in Davidson so that he could finish high school back in North Carolina. The loss of our beloved Paw Paw hit our family incredibly hard. We were already weakened from the move and the career discontent, and this sudden blow felt like more than any of us could take.

Every one of us grieved the loss, especially Nanny who had just lost her husband of fifty-plus years. And little was bright on my employment. In fact, my career was a mess, having gone from being president of a company to being asked to focus on the expertise strategy. To say that things were not going according to my plan is an understatement. The only good news is that I was starting to think about God's plan, rather than mine. Kelli and I had promised each other we would think carefully, pray hard, and discuss it fully before making any long-term decision. I respected my wife's desire to wait and not do anything under duress. We were in shock dealing with the loss of Paw Paw. This would give us time to properly analyze the situation and consider our options.

Paw Paw was the most unconditionally loving man I'd ever met in my life. Even though he had eighty-four great years none of us were prepared to say goodbye so suddenly. Sometimes when life hits you the hardest, finding humor in the difficulty can be the only thing that gets you through.

To put a cherry on top of the sundae that was my humiliation I was sharing a room in our rented apartment for Alex with my beloved mother-in-law, Nanny. We had matching twin beds like we were a couple of eight-year-olds. One night I stared at the cheap alarm clock we bought at a CVS Pharmacy, which read 3:33 A.M. Kelli's mom had woken me up again. Her nighttime breathing apparatus, which helps with her sleep apnea, had slid off her face again. It was pretty predictable like the 3 o'clock train whistling into the station. I jokingly called it the "Darth Vader" mask, because it sounded exactly like that when it was slightly off her face.

I could sleep through the deep breathing sound when the apparatus was just a little haywire. But usually in the deepest sleeping part of the night, the time when the dark is darkest, it would slide off and really make a racket. When it slid off her face just right, it made a high-pitched whistling sound like the train signaling its arrival at the station. That night I did what I normally did when this happened.

"Nanny, your mask is off," I whispered, just loud enough to wake her.

"Oh, oh. . . . Oh!" she said and moved it around, trying to get it situated.

On nights like this, the fix was only temporary. Within just a minute the mask was off kilter again and the heavy breathing and whistling was repeated. This was the first night since we had gotten the apartment in late January that I couldn't go back to sleep quickly. My mind immediately picked up in the dark spot where it had left off the night before.

Yet it was kind of funny. We'd picked up everything, ripped up the roots of centuries of family history, and moved to Georgia, thinking it was the right thing for our family. Now here I was sleeping in a small, two-bedroom apartment with my mother-in-law in one twin bed and me in the other. Matching twin beds. Just think about how small and narrow those beds are. Then picture that 240-pound body in that small space. Not naturally very comfortable.

I hoped we would all look back on this and laugh, but tonight I wasn't sure. Sometimes when you determine to be successful in your key roles you have to be willing to accept some unusual consequences. When you've truly set your top priorities as faith and family (or whatever yours are), you have to be ready to make sacrifices and set priorities to stick to it.

That day I had been helping Nanny take care of some of the estate matters and also spent time shepherding Alex as he tried to get caught up in school. I was driving from Nanny and Paw Paw's farm to our apartment in Davidson, a drive we'd made so many times over the last twenty-three years. It is a pretty drive through the country in Kannapolis and Cabarrus County on Route 3. As I was crossing over the county line into Davidson, Cami called me.

"Daddy, I want to go home. I need to be back in North Carolina. I want to be back with my brother and for all of us to be together again. Please take me home, Daddy. I don't have any friends here. I miss my friends. Please let me go home."

"I know, honey. This has been tough on all of us. I hear what you are saying to me and take it very seriously. I need to talk to Mommy and figure out what to do. For now, I need you to stay focused at school and finish strong. I love you very much. I'll call Mommy tonight. Thanks for calling me, baby."

I hung up the phone and I was overwhelmed and felt lost in the wilderness. I thought God had called me to Atlanta, but I so badly wanted to bring everyone home and circle the wagons in North Carolina. We all were missing home. I had a tremendous amount of fear when I thought about moving back. What would happen to my job and my career? A decision to move back to North Carolina would be the end of any opportunity to play a major, company leadership role or at worst might mean I'd be asked to leave. That was unlikely, but we had to consider all implications. It would clearly be a setback.

Again I felt stuck. What had I done to my family? Where were we supposed to be? I needed an answer from God and quickly. At that moment, while driving into Davidson, I cried out, *Show me! Show me! Show me, Lord!*

Immediately he gave me the craziest answer I'd ever received in my life. An image of a donkey came to me. I was completely puzzled and laughed out loud. I was amused but still needed direction. I asked God, *What does this mean?*

A few seconds later the answer came,

Mike, you will be riding on a donkey for a while . . . all the way back to Davidson, God whispered.

Strangely the donkey image was relieving. The Lord gave me what I was looking for in the form of a funny memory. As I finished my drive into Davidson I remembered that this was not the first time I'd ridden a donkey. With a big smile growing on my face I remembered back to a much simpler time.

Several years ago we had vacationed on the beaches of Daufuskie Island in South Carolina. Nanny and Paw Paw loved to go and it was really a pleasure to take them with us. The beaches on Daufuskie Island were a magical place for us. It was as if time slowed down and we had needed that. I savored every minute because of my fast-paced, time-consuming, and taxing job.

One perfect day we decided to spice it up and go horseback riding. Kelli and I took our kids, Alex, Cami, and Olivia, while Nanny and Paw Paw stayed behind at the beach house. When we arrived at the stable, everyone was given a horse or pony according to size. I was last in the selection process and clearly a challenge for the lady matching us up with our horses.

"Here you go, sir," the guide said as she handed me the reigns of a short and stout-looking horse.

"Dad, what is that?" Alex asked.

"I'm not sure," I replied with a crinkled forehead.

"Oh, that is Mike the Mule," the guide said, overhearing our conversation.

How she said it with a straight face I'm not sure. Everyone had a cream of the crop steed except me. I was handed a mule that shared my same name.

Ironic, I thought. Clearly Kelli was enjoying the moment as she had a "it couldn't get any better than this" smile. I could tell she had something she wanted to say and no words were needed.

Her white knight mounted his glorious mule.

Yes, since I exceeded the horse weight limit I needed a mule, an animal known for being able to carry heavy weight. I was humiliated but was not about to question the assignment.

We all mounted up in a straight line as we familiarized ourselves with our matched beasts. Not surprisingly, Mike was slow and steady. He was pretty short so it wasn't that scary. Mike knew where he wanted to go and didn't seem to really need my help with the process. Even if you tried you couldn't make him go off *his* course. He was a bit stubborn. Remind you of anyone else? We made our way through some of the beautiful wooded trails that eventually brought us out on the beach, following our guide in a line, with me at the back.

I looked like Fabio riding his steed triumphantly down the beach as the wind swept through my hair. Suddenly, the leader made a left turn from the beach and onto the road of our rented beachfront home. As we turned, there were Nanny and Paw Paw, sitting on the front porch. As I passed by, I will never forget Paw Paw's face, which was lit up with a smile that stretched beyond his ears.

I felt the embarrassment! He knew exactly what I was riding and thoroughly enjoyed it. Later that evening as the events of the day were obviously discussed Nanny couldn't wait to share Paw Paw's take on our procession, "That was some jackass Mike was on!"

Oh, how everybody belly-laughed and howled. Hopefully, the laughing was because the kids thought hearing Paw Paw sort of cussing was funny. Now I laughed, as well, knowing I might have just been invited into an awkward, eye-opening conversation with God. Was this humiliating ride God teaching me to focus on humility? Not sure, but it did. God does have a sense of humor and an especially good one! He is so very wise in dealing with his children.

Yes, I'm stubborn. And maybe sometimes Paw Paw's kind of cuss word… a *jackass.* And I might have looked like one not only to my family, but also to my coworkers, neighbors, and friends a time or two because of my nature and the heavy load I was carrying. Guilty as charged.

Have you acted the same? Does life sometimes seem overwhelming and bring out the worst in you?

God's promised Messiah carried the weight of our sin and the power it has over us as he rode into Jerusalem on his donkey. Humbly riding his donkey toward the cross and carrying all the extra weight we don't need to carry. He carried our stresses, our strained relationships, our bad attitudes, and our sin.

This realization put my predicament in perspective. I would gladly ride that donkey, look like a jackass, if that was what was required of me. Mike the Mule—priceless and accurate! God does have a sense of humor. A good one. I'd encourage you to do what I felt God was saying to me that day. Let's all take a load off and instead pick up an intensified devotion to the One who can carry the heavy load.

That evening, after Cami's phone call, Kelli and I discussed our daughter's desire for the family to move back to Charlotte. The first obvious thing that hit me was that my purpose was to make my faith and my family #1 and #2 priorities in my life.

My family was severely hurting because of our moving for the company. My wife was away from her grieving mother and my girls were miserable away from their friends. My first two roles of importance were husband and father. My Role Success Statements were to lead them wisely and be present in their lives. If I was wise and present at that moment, I had to see that it was in my family's best interest to go back home. My wife needed to be with her mother. They both needed it. After analyzing my current situation and my options against my Purpose and Role Success Statements I had a big "*ah hah*!"

It was time to put my career, my title, and my job on the altar and offer it to God as a sacrifice. Once I could see the manifestation of my priorities so clearly, the decision was easy. We would move back home and pay for it with our own nickel, and we would not worry about the consequences. We had 100 percent trust in God. It would be a humbling journey, but in the end, it would feel so good to make that decision for the right reasons.

Retreating is not something I was accustomed to doing. It was very humbling. I didn't know for sure if I would change jobs at this point, but I did see clearly that my family needed to be back in North Carolina. It felt good to have that clarity even though moving again would be hard and would set us back financially. It felt good to be back in the right frame of mind, focused on our top priorities of our faith and family.

During the decision-making process of whether to move to Atlanta or stay in Charlotte I hadn't relied on my Life Purpose Statement as I should have. I'd say I was caught up in the moment and too focused on making a yes-or-no decision. I would strongly recommend that you use your Life Purpose Statement all the time, and especially when you are suddenly faced with important decisions. Your Purpose Statement and your Role Success Statements should be your guideposts in making major decisions like this. Will this new job or new location help or hinder you from fulfilling your purpose and in being successful in your roles?

Do you need to recalculate your priorities? Take a moment to do so now. Follow this process and scoring system any time you feel lost or in need of guidance:

Current Situation and New Opportunity Scoring System

Evaluation against Your "Requirements"

1. Take out your Life Purpose Statement and Role Success Statements. By now I hope you have combined them onto a single piece of paper.
2. Think about the key elements contained in your Purpose Statement. For each element give yourself a score from 1—My current job/situation completely inhibits me from living out this aspect of my purpose—to 10—My current job/situation fully enables me to live out this aspect of my purpose.
3. For each of your Role Success Statements give yourself a similar score from 1—My current job/situation completely inhibits me from fulfilling this role— to 10—My current job/situation fully enables me to successfully fulfill this role.

If you are evaluating or thinking about a potential new job or situation, go through the same scoring process. This process can also be used to compare multiple job opportunities/situations to your current situation.

When I had done this process before accepting the North Highland job, my score for North Highland was an 80 and my-then current job at BearingPoint was a 35. North Highland was clearly a better fit for my purpose and my roles. However, the money offered was a little bit less. Funny thing is I'd not written anything in my Life Purpose or Role Success Statements about money, other than an implied amount needed to provide for my family.

Now this analysis helped me see that I was holding onto something for the wrong reasons, and it forced me to have integrity in the decision. Ironically, a few years later I was making more money than I ever had, but I believe it was because I was living "on purpose" and enjoying what I was doing. I fully believe if you enjoy and love what you do, and you are good at it, you will do a great job and see the fruits of your labor.

CHAPTER 8

Step Six: Find a Trainer

As You Look to the Future

Attack? Stand my ground or fight? Retreat and find another way? I was torn between how I should react to the change in my position at North Highland.

In Scripture we see there is time and a season for each approach. Should I fight for the CEO role that was used as a carrot to get us to move? Should we stay in Atlanta or head back to our home in Davidson, North Carolina? Kelli and I decided to take a month to contemplate and to pray about our options.

A while back Pastor Padilla had suggested that I find a trainer. He had used the analogy of a boxer who needs a trainer. When a boxer is busy fighting and dazed from taking hits, he cannot see his own situation very well. The boxer needs a trainer to help guide him and see more objectively what is happening.

Pastor Padilla then shared with me that I should seek out a trainer, not many, only one who is guided by the Holy Spirit. He said that too many people will have opinions on which way we should go. Some will say north, others south, and still others east and west. "You need to seek that one advisor who is guided by the Holy Spirit."

Late in March of 2014, I was excited about having an unusual Friday off from work to focus on my family and on reading and writing. I also set up some time with author Terry Lursen who I thought might be that trainer Pastor Padilla told me God would help me find. Terry published a daily devotional *The Treasures within the Kingdom of God,* which I had read for several weeks. After reading it daily I knew there was something special about this man. I believed his writing about Scripture was true and I appreciated the directness and wisdom in his words.

I found Terry's contact information through a bookstore and discovered he lived in Charlotte so I called him and set up some time to meet him there in person.

Terry and I met for coffee at Summit in Davidson, which is owned by one of Alex's former teachers who had a passion for climbing and skiing, hence the name. As I opened the front door to my familiar coffee spot, Summit Coffee, I immediately saw Terry. He was a striking-looking man with short, white hair. We exchanged smiles and greetings. There was an immediate connection. After I purchased a much-needed cup of coffee, we moved upstairs to a cozy spot where we sat in chairs that felt like you were in your own family room.

I immediately felt comfortable to share my situation with Terry in detail. I told him that I had been guilty of daydreaming about the future, because I felt God telling me to keep a daily journal of my last year's journey. What if I left my job to write the story of our experience over the last year? What if I pursued the earlier opportunities that had been coming to me in the media industry? One such opportunity was my association as a producer with the feature film *Hope's Wish*.

I had been inspired by the true story of Hope Stout, a twelve-year-old girl who was battling bone cancer when the Make-A-Wish Foundation offered her a wish. Hope's request startled the Foundation. After she was told how many other children in North Carolina were waiting to have their wishes granted, Hope replied, "Then my wish is to grant all the wishes of the 155 kids on the waiting list—every single one of them!" Her wish would cost more than one million dollars.

Miraculously that little, red-headed girl raised 1.1 million dollars in six weeks before she went to heaven. Her story and the impact it had on the city of Charlotte was being considered as a major movie.

All of these ideas greatly appealed to my creative, right-brain orientation, but I knew this was not the time to jump ship. Only being a producer for *Hope's Wish* could be done as I continued consulting.

Terry guided me to stay the course and keep focused on my job in consulting at North Highland by strongly telling me, "Don't quit your day job."

We discussed the Bible story of Jonah's mistake. Jonah did not nurture the vine that had grown up beside him, which provided shade and comfort from the desert heat. When Jonah did not take care of God's provision, this prophet burned up in the extreme heat. My vine that needed nurturing was my consulting job. My original calling from God was impressed upon me as something to continue—for now. Providing water and care to this plant was vital to my being able to afford the time to do everything else. My family needed the stability and a well, thought-out plan right now with all the changes going on in our lives. We did not need to make another hasty major change. Alex was a senior in a new high school, and Cami and Olivia were months away from finishing ninth and fifth grades respectively.

I shared with Terry my struggle to understand why God had called me to Atlanta with North Highland. From the time Dan had asked us to move, calamity had seemed to befall us. "Why have things been so hard when I thought God had clearly called me to move?"

"Is that the truth in what you saw at the time or is this the truth you realize in hindsight?" Terry asked.

His question gave me pause.

At that moment with Terry and with the benefit of hindsight, I could see things more clearly. Once presented with the opportunity to become the next CEO if we moved, I had pressed God to give me an answer— literally should we stay or go? Had I been truly seeking God's will or had I asked him to come along with my plans? My will or his will be done?

"You've heard the phrase, be careful what you pray for, right?" Terry asked.

"Yes."

"Praying for a sign from God can be dangerous. It amounts to testing God. There is a difference between praying for a specific sign or a direct answer versus praying, "Lord, your will be done."

My hands started to sweat as I contemplated if I had willed the last year into existence. I concluded that I needed to lay our future down and seek the Lord's will instead of demanding his response to my desires and questions. Had God called me to Atlanta when he said, "*Just go*" or was he giving in to my annoying, persistent questions? I had not patiently waited on the Lord back then. It was the world calling me, and I was pleading with God to give me an answer and let me go.

Now the fog of the last year was beginning to lift. I saw the sequence of the events, the prayers, the decisions, the mistakes, and all of it left out on a battlefield after a major battle. Somewhere along the path life had gotten so hard, and so out of control, we had been forced to rely on God. In hindsight I had made a mistake in pressing the Lord to show us signs of what I wanted him to tell me. I realized I shouldn't play God by praying for yes-and-no answers to questions that occur in my life.

Terry asked me to go back and tell him what had happened to North Highland two years ago. I shared the story of the Big Four firms coming back into our market and causing our business to flatten out. Revenue had been flat for two years. We were still profitable, but we needed to figure out how to get our growth engine going again. It was during this "flattening" period that I was asked to come to Atlanta. Since I had moved in June, Dan and I had worked together to reset our strategy to focus more on becoming experts in our client's business so we could counsel them better. The early results from the first quarter of this year, our first three months of operation in the new model, were promising; we were up 15 percent.

Terry really wanted me to see the fruit of Dan's decision to have me there with him. This was a good decision for Dan. My work around industries and expertise had led us to this growth, which was something I should feel good about.

"That is the fruit of obedience," Terry said. "You did the right thing for you, Dan, and for the firm. You made sacrifices, because your company needed you to do that."

"Now is the time for you to look at things from a new perspective. How is your family doing? You need to reconsider your options, Mike, in light of how Your Father in heaven views the needs of your family. What do they need? That is how you should look at it, and you need to consider your options and make wise decisions."

At this moment I realized the last year had been like a pressing process for all of us. Me, with my work; Kelli, moving away from family and friends; Alex, doing the yo-yo with his friends and school; Cami, leaving her school and friends; and Olivia, adjusting to the rigors of a harder school. We had all been pressed and flattened. God might have been molding us, testing us, and teaching us so much. Our perspective had completely changed for the better. I think we will always appreciate the little things more, like being thankful for the provision we have rather than striving for more. Being thankful for our family, our health, our job, and our home. We would make decisions differently. We would continually pray by saying, "Your will be done, Lord."

As I thought about my options I realized I had been dealing with my own real fears, fears about what might happen next. Fear of failure, fear of getting fired. I was holding onto these fears like a tree trunk in a storm as the wind swirled around me.

"The problem," Terry said, "is that the thing you are holding onto is electrified, and it is dark and not good. You've got to let go of that. You aren't stuck. You have so many options. Let go and trust God.

"Look at your family and your circumstance through the Father's eyes, Mike. Why can't you move them all back to Charlotte and travel to Atlanta a few days per week?"

I stammered as I attempted to answer his question with half-hearted justifications as to why I didn't want to do this. I didn't want to be away from my family during the work week. I didn't want to continue making the four-hour drive to Atlanta several times per month. It wore me out to think about it; I had already made that trek over 150 times, logging over 75,000 miles on I-85.

Later, as I thought about this meeting I realized the insights I gained from my time with this trainer.

1. Don't rashly quit your day job, which provides for your family.
2. Realize that the perspective of hindsight is invaluable so you can see things more clearly as you climb out of the valley.
3. Look at each of your family members through God's eyes. How does he see them and their situation?
4. A calling is not permanent. God will allow or ask you to move on. It is dangerous to be overcommitted.
5. You always have options to attack, stand your ground, retreat, or surrender. There is no dishonor in retreat or surrender when it is the right move.

This was a turning point. I could see all these observations were true. Terry was careful not to give me the answers, but to make accurate observations of what the situation was and how I was behaving in it. Even though I didn't have any definitive answers I now realized that there were options. I was no longer stuck. I had given too much control of my destiny to my fears, my job, and other people. Released from these fears I could then see the opportunity to consider all options and use the wisdom and analytical abilities God has given me to move forward confidently with the knowledge that God would move with me. No more asking for signs.

These insights and blessings came two years after we had given the Padilla's the car. As Pastor Padilla said, "If you bless a prophet, a prophet will bless you." He had given me the advice that led to the meeting with Terry and the complete 180 degree change in my outlook, perspective, and maybe most importantly my attitude. I think the lesson here is to focus on giving to others rather than focusing on our own needs. God turned around my blessing to Pastor Padilla to me through these two fine men. The spiritual lessons I've learned in return are priceless.

Terry said exactly what I needed when I had to hear the very accurate reality of my situation and my role in it. He wasn't worried about hurting my feelings. He wasn't being paid and so had nothing to lose.

In May of 2017 I asked Terry, "How have you been?" when I met with him. Terry described his last several months living in his daughter's house as "Lonely." His daughter had moved to the east coast and let him stay in her old house way out in the country while Terry and Jane prepared to sell: they had decided it was time to downsize. They had been willing to deal with some necessary, temporary separation to accommodate the move; Jane decided to stay with their son near Charlotte because she worked downtown. Terry had worked very hard on the house, which looked great inside and out. Then he had waited for the house to sell, but it wouldn't. He felt stuck, staying temporarily in his daughter's empty home. He felt alone. He couldn't even write. And he couldn't get a job despite his best efforts. Nothing was working.

It was during this time that Terry read the Bible stories of Jesus and what he would do when he was in a situation that was not productive. Terry was thinking about "going to the other side" as Jesus did so many times when he experienced rejection. Jesus didn't stay where he wasn't wanted or respected. He would leave, go somewhere else, and try again. Terry had heard from God that he needed to "go to the other side . . . to the deep water."

Through these Scriptures God showed him he needed to move out of his daughter's remote farm house and back into the nice, empty home Terry had just remodeled and hadn't sold yet. The Holy Spirit spoke to him, saying, *Move back to your home where at least you have neighbors and you won't be alone.* He did that. Moved all his stuff. Within days he got a job, then he got an offer on his house and also sold a bunch of his books, *The Treasure Within the Kingdom of God.* He was thankful to be "unstuck" and seeing positive things happen from "going to the other side."

As you can see I didn't really give Terry any advice. I just listened and that might have been what he needed at that time in his life. In late July of 2015, Terry had shifted from trainer to mentor. He and his wife, Jane, have become dear friends. I lost a trainer who can tell me what I don't want to hear, but I gained a dear friend and mentor for life.

You too can benefit from a trainer in your life. Think about that now.

Finding a Trainer

Just like in boxing you need a trainer in your life. A trainer is someone you trust and respect and ideally is someone that God puts into your life. When you go through crisis moments or periods of significant change, it is important to have someone who can see things from an objective perspective. A trainer-to-trainee relationship is impersonal and hierarchical. It is invaluable because the trainer is objective and detached from the action. In contrast the relationship is different between a mentor and a mentee, which is typically personal, confidential, and friendly. I consider Pastor Padilla a spiritual and a family mentor due to the very personal and loving nature of our friendship. I believe at different times in your life you need both a mentor and a trainer.

The trainer has many aspects of the mentor, but he or she is not as invested in the relationship and so may be more able to tell you things that a friend might worry about telling you. A trainer has a way of holding a mirror up to you, so you can see yourself more clearly.

You need someone you can be completely open with and who will give you candid input. This is such an important role that choosing the wrong trainer can significantly alter your performance and trajectory. Just like the boxing analogy—choose the wrong person and you might get knocked out. Choose wisely and you could go on to win the championship. I recommend you find someone whose advice is deeply rooted in Scripture. You want someone who asks great questions and is slow to point to solutions. This person should help you see what you need to do without telling you the answers.

So how do you find a trainer? I don't think there is a step-by-step approach to this. As Pastor Padilla told me, "You will know him when you find that person." Sometimes Pastor Padilla reminds me of Yoda from *Star Wars*. When I first hear some of his advice, I have no idea what he is talking about. Jesus was like that with the disciples. They learned much from him, but only after he had died and risen again from the dead did they fully "get it." It's like that with us too. Only with hindsight can we see the true meaning. I looked for weeks before finding Terry. I read books, I networked, and I prayed. I knew Terry was the guy that day when he was holding the mirror up to me, without telling me what to do; he was just helping me see my true self in ways that were revealing. He did it with candor. It was uncomfortable and really made me think about what I was doing. Find someone who does that for you. You will be blessed with growth through the often-painful, pruning process. It seems unfortunate but pruning is required to experience major growth.

CHAPTER 9

Step Seven: Recalibrate Your Lifestyle

Recognize Overlooked Areas that Need to Be Addressed

Back in early March of 2014, despite the major job crisis I was facing at North Highland and losing Paw Paw, our family decided to keep our commitment to go on our mission trip to San Jose, Costa Rica. Maybe getting away from home for a little while and serving, not thinking about what had happened or what might lie ahead, would do us some good. And it did. We just focused on the present and being with the Padilla's, the Wyatt's, and the children in the project.

We ended the week at the Marriot Hotel in San Jose as we had done in prior years. We were all exhausted as we checked in around 9:30 P.M., yet we had mid-morning flights the next day. Edna Wyatt approached me and said, "Mike, Pastor Padilla wants to talk with you before you go."

"I would love to, Edna, but it is very late, and I need to get Cami to bed because of her concussion," I said. Cami's doctors had cleared her for the trip with the advice for her to rest when she felt fatigued. I continued, "What if we meet early for breakfast, would that work?"

Edna told Pastor Padilla and he agreed to come back in the morning. The week was nearly over and it had been a relatively calm, spiritual experience. I went to bed that night with no idea what lay ahead in the morning. I didn't realize that God would be dealing with areas of my life that needed to be addressed. As I mentioned in chapter one when I consult with a company, I analyze the root cause of its internal financial bleeding and explore overlooked areas for a wound site. Once found we stop the hemorrhaging and bind up the wound. God and Pastor Padilla would be doing that in my life, that day.

Before Pastor arrived, I prayed, *Lord Jesus, may only your words be spoken today at this breakfast. Bind up any words that are not yours. Lord, I also pray for mercy for my family. I trust you, Lord. I also ask that you help me to be still and listen. Your humble servant and your child.*

When Pastor arrived, he began by praying, "Only your words be spoken, Lord."

The moment he said this I knew whatever happened was going to be coming from God. We had both prayed the same thing. That the Lord would speak through us and that our words would be his words. Unbelievable! This was the first time in my life I had prayed that prayer and Pastor Padilla was repeating it verbatim. I had prayed the same words ten minutes before he even arrived!

Pastor began by telling me that one morning in the middle of the past week, he had prayed from 2:00 A.M. to 4:00 A.M.

He said he had felt strongly he needed to meet with me in person rather than only pray. He had done an examination of my family and had a thought to share with me. In fact he had met with Kelli and Alex one-on-one before me. Then he mentioned an area of my life that needed to be addressed.

My Assertiveness and Impatience

Pastor Padilla used an analogy of a motorcycle to get his message across. Just as Jesus used parables, or stories, Pastor Padilla did the same. He said, "From a spiritual perspective you are like a 1000-cubic-centimeters motorcycle, the largest. Your strength, your speed, and decision making are all very high. You are flying through the avenues of life.

"The only problem is, Mike, you are not travelling alone. You have Kelli, on a 300cc bike, Alex and Cami, each on a 100cc bike, and Olivia on a 50cc motorcycle."

I laughed, remembering the time Alex almost killed himself the first time he jumped on one of those 50cc motorcycles. The memory reminded me of what could happen if one of us got ahead of the others.

When Alex was eight years old, he had become obsessed with motorcycles. Despite my fears and Kelli's protests, he convinced me to let him get the smallest motorcycle made, a Kawasaki PW-50. It looked so small and harmless that we relented. After buying it used on Craig's List, Kelli, Alex, and I took it up to Nanny and Paw Paw's farm, which had sixteen acres of area to ride. I spent about twenty minutes showing Alex how the brakes and the throttle worked and then thought he was ready for a test drive. We strapped his new helmet on and he hopped on the cycle with a huge smile on his face. He used the kick starter to crank it up and it seemed he was ready to ride. With a smile on my face I looked over to Kelli and Nanny and Paw Paw as I held the back of the bike.

"Alex, now let the clutch out like this and give it some gas," I instructed.

Suddenly the bike took off, going from zero to high speed instantly. Alex had pulled the throttle back all the way and left it there. The bike got away from me and everything seemed to go in slow motion. Alex racing ahead of me. Me sprinting to catch up. Kelli, Nanny, and Paw Paw all gasping with their mouths wide open as they were too far away to do anything. From my vantage point I was about ten yards behind, chasing the bike, and I could see a large oak tree with a five-foot-wide trunk about thirty yards ahead. Alex was headed straight for it!

I screamed, "Let go of the throttle, Alex!"

He couldn't hear me, and he definitely had forgotten what I'd just shown him.

I don't know how I did this, but somehow I caught up to him about five yards from the tree, grabbed him from behind, and yanked him to the ground. His little motorcycle continued and hit that huge tree head on.

We lay on the ground and I grimaced as I looked over and saw the look of fear on Kelli and her parents' faces. I've never felt so stupid as a father. That thirty-yard ride was the end of Alex's cycling career! I sold the bike on Craig's List the next week. This was certainly an example of me getting something on my mind, going off, and doing it without really pausing to make sure Kelli was with me. Just like this incident it rarely turned out well for me and my family. Thankfully, God protected us despite my stupidity. Pastor Padilla had certainly used an apt illustration of my assertiveness and impatience.

Without knowing about this incident, he continued with this appropriate analogy. "Because of your nature you take off and get too far ahead of your family and arrive way before anyone else. Your family says, 'Where is Mike? He passed through here.'

"You don't even slowdown in the curves," he added. To my credit he did say that when I notice that I've left them way behind, I come back.

"Kelli and the kids do not understand, and they have thousands of questions. Kelli feels lonely and not close enough to you. They wonder why you are going so fast. They want you to teach them to ride that 1000cc motorcycle. You need to know that they love you more than anything you can give them financially. You need to slow down and give up your need to be out front. Instead get behind your family and lead them from that position.

"You like to experiment," Pastor Padilla added, "but don't leave your caravan behind you. If you lose your family, you are a failure."

After pausing to let that analysis sink in, he continued, "Very soon all that is messed up in your job situation will be straightened and the things that you don't know will be revealed to you. Your questions will be answered. God himself will guide you. He will open doors and close doors. He will take you where you need to be. He will give you great peace and a great gift, a gift greater than fame and fortune and better than anything worldly you could be given. It is the grace of God over you, Mike."

At this point I started losing it. God's mercy washed over me. It had been so hard taking care of everyone after losing Kelli's dad and trying to keep everybody together while my position in North Highland seemed so precarious.

As I cried Anais, Pastor Padilla's wife, reached over and put her hand on my back. I knew it was the hand of God, the great comforter touching me through her.

As Anais gently rubbed my back, Pastor Padilla continued, "The Holy Spirit is giving you a gift, Mike. It is the gift of knowledge and wisdom. This blessing is for you and for your family. From this moment the Lord's heaven will move through you. You will know how to fix the problems facing your family, Kelli, and the children. You will be guided by the Holy Spirit in all your decisions.

"Mike, do you know what your problem is?"

I shook my bowed head, "No."

"It is not your company, your family, or you. Your problem is time. With the gift of knowledge/wisdom you will be able to discern which things you should spend your time on and which ones you should not. You will need to slow down from 1000cc to 300cc in order to take the time to see these things more clearly. You are normally like a mouse that sees many pieces of cheese and wants to go after all of them. You will now be able to focus on the cheese you are supposed to spend your time on.

"From now on you will see your family and your company very differently. You will enjoy your life and let God take you where he wants you to go. Remember, though, you must lose something to win something. Your new knowledge will help you determine what is good and what is bad. Every day I want you to read a chapter in the Book of Proverbs. This wisdom will implant itself in your mind like a machine."

Then he asked me if I had any questions.

"How do I know where God wants me to go? Right now I am not sure."

Pastor Padilla shared a Bible story about Abraham. During Abraham's life he and his tribe followed a cloud, which was from God. If the cloud moved, they moved the whole tribe. After Abraham died the cloud disappeared, and Abraham's son did not know where to go. God told him you don't need the cloud anymore, because wherever you go I am with you.

To make his point Pastor Padilla said, "Mike, do you know how God came to be here right now, in this Marriot Hotel this morning?"

Again I shook my head, "No."

"He came with you, Mike! He will be on that airplane with you, because you are bringing him with you."

Pastor Padilla continued. "Mike, you don't need to worry about where you are going. God will be with you, no matter where you are or where you go. Trust him and he will lead you. When your plane lands in Atlanta, you will have an answer from God."

I would count this meeting as the most incredible spiritual experience of my life. To me Pastor Padilla is one of the "giant men in the faith." His heart for God always captivates me.

Later that morning we had a wonderful flight back home and I sat next to Cami. She drew and wrote in her journal, and I finished the book *To Heaven and Back: A Doctor's Extraordinary Account of Her Death, Heaven, and Life Again.* A true story by Dr. Mary C. Neal.

As we were completing our final descent I was reading about how this doctor recovered from a major kayaking accident in which she died, went to heaven, and then returned. She was in her hospital bed and was flipping through the Bible. She was frustrated because she could not read any of it, because her brain was still injured from the lack of oxygen. Then all of a sudden one verse was crystal clear to her....

Just as the wheels of our Delta jet plane touched down I read:

"*Rejoice Always.*"—1 Thessalonians 5:16 (ESV)

There it was as Pastor Padilla predicted: an answer from God in heaven. It is the same message Kelli had received while praying after the loss of her father a month ago, before we left for Costa Rica when she was given,

"*This is the day that the Lord had made; We will rejoice and be glad in it*"[2]

If you are anything like me, you must learn things the hard way. I'm a control freak by nature. It's why consulting has been a good calling for me; we try to think of everything to control a great outcome for our clients. We call it excellent project management, others call it control freakiness! You can spend weeks, years, or even decades trying to go your own way. I've learned the hard way that the best years of my life have come from surrendering to God. No one can do this for you. You must decide you are going to give up control of what happens next and be obedient to what the Lord asks of you. It's the simplest and hardest thing you'll ever do. Surrender to God and ask, "Show me, Lord, what you want me to do."

Pastor Padilla had shown me the first area of my life that needed to be addressed: my assertiveness and impatience. The second adjustment was pride, which didn't occur until 2018, but I had begun to realize this fault during my job changes in 2014.

My Pride

After we made the decision to move back to North Carolina in August of 2014, our family had experienced a feeling of great relief. It was hard to pack up again and move everybody back but we were all 100 percent in support of the decision. Kelli would be home in Davidson near her mother, Cami and Olivia would be back with their friends, and even Alex was supportive as he preferred to spend his summers when not in college back in Davidson with his friends. Life on the family front was hectic, but we were all happy with the new direction we were heading.

However, my work life was a whole different story. We had moved back to North Carolina, still with North Highland. I continued to work hard to launch our new expertise offerings for my company as I had been asked. I enjoyed building the things that were critical to our future survival, growth, and profit; however I was disappointed with not running the core business. The humbling issue was that I was being pushed out of the "real" leadership of the company. Increasingly the CEO would lean on others to make changes he knew I did not agree with.

When you are in a situation where you don't agree with the CEO or your boss, you have two choices: go to the Board of Directors, over his/her head, or leave. I made the decision that I would not be with the company much longer unless something major changed, but I was weighing how to deal with it. Losing direction of a company that I'd helped build from the ground up was very difficult. And having been asked to move to Atlanta to be a successor, and then having the rug pulled out from under me as we unpacked, was a very hard pill to swallow. In these difficult times I tried so hard to keep up the good fight, to show up for our people, and to have a good attitude. I felt dejected, wounded, betrayed, and misled. It was during these hard times that Kelli reminded me to do the best I could in the situation and I was also given a Scripture that stays with me to this day. When all else fails, when you feel lost, unmotivated, look to Micah 6:8: "And what does the Lord require of you but to do justly, to love mercy, and to walk humbly with your God?"[3] When all else fails this is our job description for work and for our lives. I keep it etched in my mind and even went so far as to have it carved into the stone foundation of our home.

Kelli knew very well that I was unhappy, and that I was struggling to find a way to make it work. After twelve years with the company and a strong track record for growth and profit, I did not want to just walk away without trying everything I could think of to fix it. I made numerous presentations to the CEO about my observations and recommendations, but they largely fell on deaf ears.

Sometimes when the platform is burning you'd better jump off into the water before you get burned or it blows up and kills you. I was badly singed. My hair was a little on fire and I was already going to have scars from the heat.

Picture a guy with soot all over his skin and face and his hair standing on end with smoke floating from the split ends. Sound a bit dramatic? Maybe. But I was that frustrated by what was happening and my inability to control what was going on. I felt I could not fix this on my own.

This is a bad feeling, but ironically a very good thing. It forced me to my knees, confessing and pleading with Jesus, *Lord, I can't do this on my own. I need your help to get out of this. Please show me what to do. I turn it over to you.*

God answered by helping me to find things in my heart, dark places in my life. The years between March of 2014 and May of 2018 were a period of much needed house cleaning. The first step had been addressing my lack of humility. Now my excessive pride needed to be realized. This would ultimately be a good thing as it would force me to name this fault and deal with it with the Lord's help and help from my wife, a friend, and Terry.

Pride is the opposite of humility. Pride is 100 percent a spiritual sin and can therefore be difficult to see in ourselves, even though it's easy to spot in others. It is the most terrible tool of the devil and is in fact the thing that made Satan who he is: a fallen angel who thought he was better than God or that he could be equal with God.

Back in 2013 and 2014 the humiliation I experienced in moving, losing my role as overall president of the company, seeing my family suffer, and not being able to fix it on my own had in fact done some good. It began to force me to see my issue with pride, which had multiple layers.

First, my natural ability to drive projects to successful completion when overdone can manifest itself as pride. As consultants we are trained to figure out creative solutions to complex problems. When one way doesn't work, we re-diagnose, come up with a new plan, and try again. The problem is when I think I can figure it out on my own, without God's help or inspiration, I open myself to the sin of pride.

My pride was finally broken on Saturday, May 26, 2018, an incredible day. I met with Terry for the second time in a week, and he was forcing me to dig deep into why I wasn't feeling happy. *Hope's Wish*, the important charitable movie project I'd thought was God-ordained, had crashed.

It looked like the best-case scenario was a year's delay. I was frustrated but I couldn't see how much this was affecting me. That is until Terry held up that figurative mirror to me again. I'd had several days since our first meeting that week to ponder his question, "What is deeper, Mike, what is really bothering you?"

I had the time, by myself, to go through the notes of my conversations with Terry. I found the part where he commented on my demeanor the last two times I'd met with him. He observed that I'd looked defeated and dejected; I'd told him I was worried about my business and was not happy with how the charitable movie project was going—it was failing.

In 2011 I had made a decision to invest in the early development of *Hope's Wish*. The decision to invest back then was another moment where God straightened me out. We had met Hope's mom and dad, Shelby and Stuart Stout, at one of our daughter Cami's cheer competitions. The Stouts had asked for our help raising funds for the film. They needed enough to hire talented, screenplay writers. I agreed to help, thinking I could find business contacts that might have a heart for the project.

One day, as I drove down Independence Boulevard in Charlotte, I was thinking about calling on a successful business friend of mine who had plenty of resources to pull this off. As I thought about him putting his hard-earned money into this potentially risky investment I thought, *How can I ask my friend to put his hard-earned money into the project when I haven't put any of our money into it?* This was when God had a stern word with me. It was like he hit me in the head with a two-by-four. He said, *That is not your money, Michael, it is my money! Everything you have is mine, not yours. I've given it all to you. Your money, your family, your house, your car. All of it. Every breath you take.*

I was stunned by the thought and knew I needed to act before anything or anyone changed my mind. I picked up the phone and called my buddy Stuart, Hope's daddy, and agreed to invest in the screenplay development. This got the ball rolling again and Diana Ossana, who won an Oscar for writing *Brokeback Mountain*, agreed to write the script.

It took us seven years, but in 2018 we were on the verge of turning Hope's incredible story of unselfishness into a major motion picture. *The Hollywood Reporter* and *The Charlotte Observer* had both announced that Queen Latifah had signed on to play the

Make-A-Wish Foundation granter who worked with Hope to help raise the money.

Then in April we had been dealt a very difficult blow. After a major film company promised to make her movie and had been working on pre-production for several months, the company suddenly pulled the plug without an explanation. We had invested years in getting to that point and it was so hard to accept that it had fallen apart. We were absolutely devastated for the Stout's.

We had tried everything humanly possible to help them make the movie, and we felt it was unfair to see it unfolding in this way. After working so hard at it I was taking this as a personal failure.

Terry now helped me to see that I had to let go of my need for the successful completion of projects. I had made accomplishment an idol. God had asked Kelli and me to invest in the project. He did not tell us what would happen after that. He required obedience and that was all. He made no other promises about what would happen afterward. The idea that it should happen now was mine. Again, it was my will rather than his will.

I suddenly realized that God is pleased with our obedience and our relationship with him, not necessarily with our accomplishments. He says, "Well done, good and faithful servant" when we are simply obedient. Terry had held the mirror up to me, and now I could see the ugly face of pride in accomplishments staring back at me. Rather than keep my identity in Christ I had let pride creep in, and accomplishments had become an idol. I had been pushing too hard for the movie to happen in the way I thought was right. He called us to invest, but not to micromanage the process. I needed to let go.

I needed to repent and turn from my old ways of thinking to a new way of thinking: seeking the mind of Christ. Here are my verbatim notes from this moment. . . .

Old Way	**New Way of Thinking**
I placed accomplishment, titles, success, esteem, and pursuits ahead of all – even using God's calling as an excuse. My outlook of joy vs. sadness was tied to accomplishments and how my projects were going.	Jesus is calling us to be more like him, to follow him. He abides in me and I can bask in his presence at any time. I will put him first every day, every moment. My identity is in Jesus, not accomplishments.
God called me to do important work so I gave it my all– with our time, our money, and our resources. My will was very strong. I often felt justified because God had called me. I added my own ideas to what God had told me.	God called me with specific instructions, but those instructions did not include forcing my will on the way something should turn out or forcing a timeframe for it.
If things didn't go my way, I would get upset, angry, manipulative, and pushy. I would feel dejected and let down.	I will place only my relationship with Jesus as #1. If something fails or doesn't go the way I want, I will not make that #1. Jesus is the main thing. Period.
I would fight like David if someone or something resisted me.	I will be like Jesus who took his teaching, his message, his power "over to the other side." He went somewhere else where he was welcome. You can't force people to do things they don't want to do.

The next Sunday I went forward at the end of our church service to let go of the charitable movie project that I'd been holding on to so tightly. I prayed, *Lord, I can't do this anymore. I release this project to your hands. Your will be done, Lord, not mine. In the name of Jesus. Amen.* I immediately felt released from this bondage. A huge weight was lifted.

I'm not saying pride in accomplishment doesn't creep back up now and then, but I can spot it, name it, confess it, and pray for forgiveness and deliverance in Jesus' name. Pride died the day it was revealed to me. I thank Jesus for the discernment and for taking it from me. In some strange way it felt so good to get to this point. I felt a kinship with my Lord and his rejection and humiliation. Ironically the hardest things to deal with have led to the best feeling of my life—feeling one with my Jesus. His humility, his sacrifice, his love, his grace, and his unfailing mercy.

Now I needed to revisit my Life Purpose Statement again. For the third time in my life I went to Step 2:

Our Life Purpose: To lead our family, business, and resources in a way that honors God and reflects the love, joy, and peace of Jesus and to passionately help others find an amazing purpose-driven life.

It was time to be intentional about declaring what Kelli and I were going to be about. I waited for inspiration.

By the grace of God I've had the issues of pride and over assertiveness revealed to me. Scripture promises us that anything is possible in his name. What are you holding on to that you need to confess to the Lord and turn over to him?

Periodic Housecleaning

Take an honest look at yourself and recognize and confess your need. You must stop pretending everything is alright. What people call salvation is simply the first stage of God's ultimate plan for our lives, which is to conform us in character and power to the image of Jesus Christ. If we fail to see our relationship to God accurately, we will allow too many areas within us to remain unchanged. Scripture calls these areas strongholds. My layman's version of a stronghold is this: any sin or bad-thought pattern that gives the enemy (the devil) entrance into our minds, our thoughts, and thereby our lives. Any area of our heart or mind that is not surrendered to Jesus is vulnerable to this kind of attack.

Only when we are willing to humble ourselves and admit we need help from Jesus will our deliverance from our strongholds come. In his book, *The Three Battlegrounds*, Francis Frangipane defines strongholds as "the spiritual fortresses wherein Satan and his legions hide and are protected. These fortresses exist in the thought-patterns and ideas that govern individuals and churches, as well as communities and nations. Before victory can be claimed, these strongholds must be pulled down and Satan's armor removed. Then the mighty weapons of the Word and the Spirit can effectively plunder Satan's house."[4] In consulting terms we might call them overlooked areas in a wound site. Once found, we stop the hemorrhaging and bind up the wound. That's what I needed to do now.

Frangipane gives a potential list of strongholds: pride, fear, failure, experiences, wrong doctrine, impatience, and control. You will note that several of these strongholds have occurred in my life and I know there is potential for them to crop up in the future.

I have asked the Lord to help me identify these strongholds when I am susceptible to them and help me replace them with the presence of Jesus. How about you?

Take a moment now to identify your strongholds. Review my list on the previous page. This would be a great conversation to have with your trainer. The Scriptures say that we must attain "humility of mind." We must humble our hearts and repent, exercising our faith in God to change us. If there is a habit of sin in one's life that area becomes the dwelling place for the enemy to rob a person of power and joy. Being honest with yourself will likely take the help of a counselor or a trainer. Often times these areas are well hidden from us, like my issues of assertiveness and pride. What habits do you want to break? The enemy does not want you to identify them or confess them as sin. That is why you need to do exactly that. Don't hide them. Confess them to a loved one and most importantly confess them to God.

Your Strongholds:

____

____

____

____

Now that you have identified these dark spots or sore spots and you've confessed them to God you are ready to be freed from them. Pray this with me....

Dear Heavenly Father, I confess my sin of

____

Thank you for helping me see it. I turn this area of my thinking and actions over to you. I give it to Jesus who makes all things new. In the mighty name of Jesus I ask you to free me from this bondage, and I ask you to demolish this stronghold and replace it with the joy, peace, and love of Jesus. Amen.

CHAPTER 10

Step Eight: Look Forward to Your Journey

Be Willing to Take a Risk

In the spring of 2015, as Kelli and I waited for an answer to our prayers for direction on my job, our family went on vacation with the kids to Wild Dunes near Charleston, South Carolina, where I read the book *Life Mastery* by Bob Shank. In the middle of the book the author asks the question, “What is the greatest source of your discontent, pain, and suffering?” I wrote my job dissatisfaction and frustration in the blank line.

Then the writer asked, “What is the one thing you are going to do tomorrow to make a change in that area?”

“Resign,” I wrote. It was a beautiful, blank sheet of paper for me and my family.

Then I immediately looked at our Life Purpose Statement and began the process of thinking about a new future.

Four weeks later I was without a job for the first time in my adult life. Thankfully we had enough savings to take some time to consider our next move. I'd been working for someone else for twenty-five years. My dream had been to start my own company, but I didn't even consider it or bring it up with Kelli since we had encountered so much trouble with the move to Atlanta for my career. How could I do that to my wife? I felt I was like marathon runners who after running 26.2 miles collapse at the finish line, exhausted and dehydrated. The medical team wraps them in an aluminum blanket and rolls those runners over to the side.

I thought I might take a few months off before jumping back into work. I don't like sitting idle, but I wanted a little more time to recuperate and to contemplate life and our next move. God had different plans. "No rest for the weary," as they say. Looking back on the situation I can see what God was doing with me.

On the morning of June 20, 2015, two weeks after I made my resignation from the company official, my wife came to me and said, "I was on my knees praying this morning and I felt the Lord tell me that you need to legally get a company set up, because your friends are going to call. You need to be prepared."

It blew me away for two reasons. First, I'd never received such specific instructions on what I needed to do in my professional work from God through Kelli. Second, the fact that Kelli was telling me to do something so risky as start a company with our own funds after what we had been through was shocking to say the least. For that reason, I knew this was not Kelli's idea. This is not something she would ever come up with on her own. Not after what we'd been through. Pastor Padilla had taught us that when God speaks, you have six seconds to say, "Yes, Lord."

During our trip to Costa Rica in 2014, he had told Kelli, that the next calling would come to her, not me. He was right. He had taught me about obedience to God two years ago. At that time he had shaken my world when he challenged my weakness to obey. He said to me, "You have six seconds to obey God when he speaks to you."

"Six seconds? . . . How long does that give me to do anything? Can't I think about it for a few days?"

Disobedience to God is not on my to-do list. Ever. With that being said, I realized I needed to work through my mentor's challenge at all costs. My heart had been convicted.

As I laser focused on my "six seconds" I quickly learned "studies and research of scientists and mathematicians have found *a present moment hardly exceeds five seconds.*"[5] In other words, I have a mere "moment with God."

Then I better get busy battling for the future that God is orchestrating through my obedience. My future, my family's future, and other people's future might rest on one obedient moment. I am not being overly dramatic. This is real-life stuff.

Let's be clear. I'm not talking about making rash decisions on issues that require godly counsel, prayer, or fasting. These practices are crucial and should never be missed. I am talking about immediately obeying God once he has broken through to your heart and has made his plans clear to you without a shadow of a doubt. You have six seconds to say, "Yes, Lord," before that present moment passes by.

A missed moment can be costly to your family and others, your destiny, and God's kingdom. Lost opportunities, unreached souls, squandered provision, and a lack of peace are too costly to risk disobedience. Obedience is always on my mind.

Think about how it feels as a parent when we give our children instructions, and they say "No" or "Let me think about that and get back to you." I can tell you as a dad it doesn't feel too good. We expect our children to listen to us.

In 1 Samuel 13, Saul and his troops were gearing up to go into battle. They had been waiting a week for Samuel to arrive and offer a sacrifice before they headed into war. Saul eventually grew impatient for the prophet to show up, so he disobeyed the Lord and offered his own sacrifice.

When Samuel arrived soon after, he rebuked King Saul: "What is more pleasing to the LORD: your burnt offerings and sacrifices or your obedience to his voice? Listen! Obedience is better than sacrifice, and submission is better than offering the fat of rams. So because you have rejected the command of the LORD, he has rejected you as king."[6]

Saul's rush to sacrifice on his own terms due to impatience (disobedience) ended in the sacrificing of his very throne. Obedience revives our hearts; disobedience can certainly nosedive careers, marriages, circumstances, and anything dear to us.

Obedience is a powerful weapon. Saul let his weaknesses of prideful impatience and distrust lead his decision to disobey. His disobedience teaches us that the weakest part of our heart rules if we let it. Yet we don't have to succumb to the lies, idols, doubt, insecurities, or any other weak part of our heart. We can be people *who will do all his will* the moment God speaks.

Our moments with God become monumental when we allow him to revive our hearts by healing our wounds, renewing our minds, and strengthening our resolve to obey. Certainly Kelli's moment with God was monumental in our lives. At her encouragement I got the legal process started for our own company, but I didn't have the energy/fire in my belly that I knew would be required. I had poured blood, sweat, and tears into building North Highland for twelve years and after the way it ended I was emotionally and physically exhausted. It was hard to say goodbye to something I'd believed in and spent over a decade building.

We had also moved twice in one year and lost Kelli's dad. In moments of doubt I would think, *I'm not 33 this time around. I'm too old at forty-seven to pull this off.*

Yet it had been a dream of mine to start a company. Looking back on my career I had enjoyed the early growth years in Arthur Andersen Business Consulting and then helping to build North Highland. Once again, I realized that God had prepared me, given me the experience over the last twenty-five years, and the unique abilities to do what he would call me to do next. It was beautiful, ironic, and necessary that he speak directly to Kelli regarding our next assignment. Starting a business from scratch with your own resources is scary, fun, exciting, and risky. "All that and a box of chocolates," as Forest Gump said in the movie by the same name.

With Kelli's blessing and encouragement, we could weather the ups and downs as a team. So I found a great North Carolina lawyer to help named Cathy Bentz. She is a no-nonsense, competent attorney who runs a small and efficient legal factory called Bentz and Associates. She is so efficient she won't even have a cup of coffee with her clients. She is a "make it happen" kind of person and I love her for it.

I scheduled a meeting with her and asked what I should bring. "You need to bring a check to the state of North Carolina for $400, and you need to have a name for the company." It was a Friday and the meeting was set for the next Tuesday. We were launching a new consulting company inspired by God and it needed a name.

That weekend I engaged my wife and children in the naming process and even started thinking about logos. Looking back we came up with some funny and terrible names. Hudson Consulting was the favorite of our youngest daughter, Olivia, because she thought it sounded sophisticated like Nordstrom's. Cardinal, Blue Sky, Davidson, Connect Consulting, Red Bird, and Mainstreet were among the brainstormed names that fell on the cutting-room floor. We had fun with the process, but nothing was seriously sticking.

On Sunday night I went to sleep a little stressed out, because none of the names were clicking. At 4:00 A.M. on Monday morning I sat up in bed wide awake with the name in my head: Independence Consulting. The name was etched in my brain like God had written it there—Independence Consulting!

So many times, when I am working on a difficult client project, my mind will continue to work while I'm sleeping. I only charge fixed-fee assignments, so I don't have to worry about whether to bill my clients for this time. They get the "dream work" as part of the package.

On one global project in January of 2017, I woke at 2:00 A.M. in London with a perfectly calculated way to save over $15 million by shifting the locations where the company's tasks are performed. I had quickly scribbled the complex tables and calculations in my journal and then went back to sleep.

With Independence Consulting ringing in my head I got out of bed and went to the kitchen in our small rental house. I fired up my computer and Googled "Independence Consulting." I was shocked to see that it was for sale for only $750; the website had a button that said, "Buy it now." I resisted the urge and decided to open another window and Googled "Freedom Consulting," which was also available, but for twenty thousand dollars! I quickly went back to the other screen and clicked "Buy it now." It looked like it went through.

For several minutes I enjoyed sipping my cup of coffee, until I got an email from GoDaddy where I had purchased the domain name. "Dear Mr. Lee, there seems to be a problem with your order of www.independenceconsulting.com. Please call us immediately to resolve this matter."

My heart sank. Since our minds so often can go to the worst-case scenario, I now convinced myself that we would not be getting this domain name. I knew it seemed too good to be true! Yet it seemed providential that the name came to me and that it was available for such a reasonable price. It was not yet even 6:00 A.M., and I decided to drive to Summit Coffee so I wouldn't wake the family while I responded to GoDaddy.

As I drove to the coffee shop I dialed the number on Bluetooth. "Hello, I'm calling regarding my recent purchase of a domain that I received an error message about. The email instructed me to call in."

After I gave the representative my order number, this is what I heard: "Yes, Mr. Lee, I see your order here right now. It looks like it is hung up in the system for some reason. I'll need to do some checking with the service that owns this site. Please hold."

I heard some typing and "*Hmmm*. . . . Okay, . . . Let's see. . . . *Aa, ahhh*. Yes, Mr. Lee, I have good news. The purchase has now gone through. You own it."

"Thank you so much," I replied.

"You are very welcome, Mr. Lee. Wow! You really got a good name. Independence Consulting. It's very unusual to find a domain like that with a full name spelled out for a price like that."

"I know. I saw that Freedom Consulting cost over twenty thousand dollars," I replied.

"It is like this name just fell out of the clear blue sky and right into your lap!"

"Yes, guess you could say that," I said laughing, thinking about how God's hand was all over this. The representative couldn't see my reaction over the phone, but I smiled as I watched the sun rise over Main Street, Davidson. Then I shared the story of what God had done that morning with that representative. A new day was dawning.

The name had strong meaning on two different levels. First, to me and my family, because it represented striking out on our own and starting a family business from scratch. We had started and grown businesses before, but not on our own with our own money.

Yes, we would be taking a big risk, but we would have the freedom to build our company with strong conviction for good values and culture, always doing the right thing for our clients and our people—no matter the cost. It would also give us the opportunity to fully integrate our faith into the way we would work as a company. We would treat our clients and our employees in a way that honored God. People from all faith, ethnic, and gender backgrounds would be welcome and could expect to be treated with respect and dignity. We would be able to be business leaders who are also Christians.

For the record, I've never talked to someone about Jesus at work who didn't ask me about my faith. I've believed that the best way we make Jesus known in the world is to follow his instructions for living. Jesus didn't walk around talking about himself. He loved people, he healed people, he fed people, he taught people, and he served people. Rather than ram our faith down someone else's throat we would try to make him known by building credibility through doing great work for clients and by treating them and our people the way God expects us to: honestly, fairly, selflessly, and with love. We would lead by example and be accountable to ourselves and God for our behavior. God is the giver of freedom. He would be our new direct supervisor!

Secondly, the name had special meaning in the consulting industry. One of the big lessons learned after the autopsy of Enron's and Arthur Andersen's failure was the conflict of interest caused by auditors also doing consulting work for their audit clients. How could auditors be truly independent and objective on an audit when they were making more money doing consulting work? Would they be able to put their lucrative consulting fees at risk if they needed to give a client an unfavorable audit opinion? In the case of Enron it was deemed to be a root cause for why Arthur Andersen did not highlight and address the risks in Enron's business faster.

That was in 2001/2002. In the wake of that crisis all but one of the large and mid-sized accounting/audit firms sold off their consulting businesses. Fast forward to 2018 and all of the large accounting firms have rebuilt consulting operations to where they are multi-billion dollar pieces of their business.

I believe this is a bad business model as it is fraught with inherent conflict of interests. Audit firms are doing consulting work for their audit clients again. Yes, they do have new restrictions and approvals that they must follow, but it still creates a conflict. I believe that audit and consulting businesses should be separate to maintain the integrity of the audit and accounting profession.

Money and profitability are the motivators for the audit firms to build these lucrative businesses. History will repeat itself and this conflict of interest will do damage to our financial markets, the investors, and our country again. I therefore believe that clients need a consultant who is 100 percent clear of any perceived or real conflict of interest.

Have we learned nothing from the tragic collapse of Arthur Andersen and Enron?

I guess not.

Two days after my conversation with the GoDaddy representative, we registered Independence Consulting as a company in North Carolina. The paperwork would be expedited, signed, and sealed on July 5, 2015, the day after Independence Day for the United States of America. The United States of America had a birthday on July 4, 1776 and two hundred and thirty-nine years later we celebrated the birth of Independence Consulting.

Think back with me to the goals I set before I joined North Highland. Let's look at what I answered to the fifteen-years-from-now questions. Under the question "What could I be doing then?" I wrote, "I could be starting or running my own company in a way that creates a strong business culture and set of values and makes a difference in the lives of others."

And in response to the question, "What might people say about you?" I wrote, "I could be taking risks and pursuing passions at work and through charities." James Wyatt and I and our families had founded the ministry One by One in Costa Rica.

I seemed to be right on track.

Yet I was still not feeling 100 percent ready for the incredibly hard work it would take to start a business again. There are often difficult financial decisions. Sell the car? Dip into savings? Cancel vacations? Take on debt? These are all decisions we would have to make in order launch and sustain the company in its infancy. It is a whole different ballgame when your own money is being put at risk. With three kids, either in college or getting ready for it, we took a deep breath and pushed off from the dock. Through it all God still provided.

He speaks to us in many ways. You will know when he tells you. The most important parts of this process are to:

1. Submit this process and your life to God. Pray that he would show you the way in his timing, not yours. Pray, "Lord, your will be done."
2. Wait on the Lord to speak to you: through Scripture, through prayer, through circumstances.
3. Be obedient when he gives you direction. According to Pastor Padilla you have six seconds to say yes when he calls.
4. Remember to have fun and be yourself. God will go with you, no matter what. Even when you make a wrong turn, you can always make a U-turn or change course.

CHAPTER 11

Step Nine: Determine to Do What's Right

Use Your Life Experiences to Plan Ahead

During the next week I made plans to work with my former mentor, Terry Lursen, on writing a business plan and envisioning our company values. That Sunday Kelli asked me if I would stay with Nanny in Kannapolis as she was having a hard time staying there by herself. I was happy to do this as Nanny and I enjoy reading books together. This helped keep her mind occupied while alone, now that Gene was gone.

We watched *The Price Is Right* together, read our separate books, and had a goodnight's sleep. In the morning Nanny made a big country breakfast with scrambled eggs, country ham, and biscuits, which may have been the other reason I was happy to stay.

That morning I was excited to begin the specific planning for our company. I drove from Kannapolis back toward Huntersville to meet with my mentor at his house. I was on a back-country road I'd been on hundreds of times before and had Terry's address plugged into my iPhone map application. The phone was sitting on the passenger seat.

As I approached the intersection of Windy Road my phone lit up and displayed "left turn." I went to make the turn, and as soon as I got into the opposite lane I saw a silver car emerge on the road ahead from under the branches of a very large oak tree. Immediately I realized I'd messed up and I corrected my car back into my lane.

Unfortunately, the driver of the silver car had already corrected into my lane. *CRUNCH!* We met head-on in the middle of the road. He was going about fifty miles per hour and I was probably going about ten miles-per-hour as I was turning. It was like hitting a wall at sixty miles per hour. At this point everything went in slow motion.

The left front of my Audi A6 hit his left front. The hood of my car folded up as the entire engine area of the car squeezed together like an accordion. Because of the angle of the crash my airbag did not deploy, which gave me a great view of what was happening. I was stunned, but immediately leaped from the car to check on the other driver.

After hitting me head-on, his car had glanced off mine and ended up in the ditch on the other side of the road. I was so worried he was seriously hurt. I could tell as I approached that his airbag had gone off and that he was dazed but breathing and mumbling. I laid a hand on his shoulder and prayed, crying out, "Lord, please, please heal this man. Lord, I pray that there is nothing wrong with him and that he will be completely healed!"

As I prayed he opened his eyes, even though he was still groggy. I said, "I'm so sorry. That was completely my fault. Are you okay? What can I do for you?"

He thanked me for taking responsibility and I chatted with him until the police and the ambulance arrived. (He would come through the accident without any major injury and so did I.)

I was groggy from the collusion, but I was fired up to stick to writing our business plan. I had an overwhelming feeling that the enemy Satan did not want me to succeed. This made me even more determined. As the ambulance pulled off and the tow truck arrived to take the black metal heap that used to be my car, I called Terry Lursen and said, "Terry, it's Mike. I was in an auto accident but I'm okay. Can you come pick me up? I'm standing on the corner of Windy Road and Route 3."

That afternoon I worked with Terry to start a business plan for Independence Consulting. The process began with defining the values for the company. From all that I had experienced at Arthur Andersen and North Highland I believed strongly that clearly articulating our values would be the foundation on which everything would be built.

These values came quickly to me as I'd been dreaming of the kind of company we might want to create for years. I didn't know what type of work we would do, but I knew what I wanted it to feel like to work with Independence Consulting, either as an employee or as a client.

Over the two weeks leading up to the writing of our company values, I had been particularly thinking about my experience at Arthur Andersen.

During trying times, like the dissolution of Arthur Andersen, character gets tested. You get to see what people are made of. Many employees were brave and selflessness; I saw truth telling, transparency, and perseverance. Unfortunately, as in any disaster when character is tested you are going to see people behave poorly as well. Traits like self-preservation, selfishness, greed, lying, and gossip were also exhibited. It is like when a pond gets drained empty and you get to see everything that has been hiding at the bottom. In this case there were some real treasures and unfortunately there was a lot of ugly junk too.

The Enron and Arthur Andersen collapses are both epic case studies in how deterioration in a company's values and ethics and the creation of a toxic culture can kill a company. I'm not talking about values that are put on posters and in company sales literature. I'm talking about values truly lived out by people who care deeply about doing the right thing in all they do. I can't speak to Enron and what happened there, but it appears that extreme pride, greed, and lack of transparency was all rampant at Andersen.

I had started my career at Arthur Andersen, doing audit work for three years and consulting for nine years with dozens of clients. I knew the firm's history, and I was indoctrinated in its stated values upon joining during a two-week training session. The man Arthur Andersen was revered in the accounting world for always "doing the right thing," no matter the consequence. He was known to walk away from clients if he did not agree with the propriety of their accounting methods. He created a culture where his employees and partners were encouraged to do the same: "Do the right thing" for your client, their investors, and their employees. The firm grew because clients and the markets knew they could trust a set of financial reports signed by Arthur Andersen.

The company did not fail because the government indicted them for their role in the Enron downfall, even though that is technically accurate. Arthur Andersen failed because the culture and values of the company had deteriorated as the firm grew.

Early in my time with Arthur Andersen I couldn't see this clearly, but with twelve years there and the last fifteen years with North Highland I had insights that only came with the perspective of hindsight. From all I'd seen and learned I can tell you for certain the firm failed because of a failure in maintaining and nurturing good culture and values.

Please do not misunderstand me. There were many great people at the firm who lived out the good values throughout their entire career. However, at some point in the firm's history the culture shifted. In my experience this typically happens as new leadership takes the reigns, and it can be a slow fade over decades. The bottom line, though, is the firm I was a part of was so focused on growth and profit and "being the best" that they lost collective sight of the most important focus: "Do the right thing" for their clients and their people. While I was there it wasn't easy to spot, but there were moments upon reflection where you could see the real priorities were off kilter.

Yet there were people in the firm who continued to "Do the right thing." As we all suffered through the indictment of Andersen, Gene Frauenheim, my office managing partner (OMP), was doing all he could to help the firm he had worked for his whole adult life. He was asked to go back to Houston after David Duncan, the Arthur Andersen auditor in charge of the Enron Audit as Houston's OMP, was fired for shredding audit documents in the days after Enron failed. Gene was a Texan through and through who had been relocated from Houston years earlier to Charlotte to lead Arthur Andersen's fast-growing practice in the Carolinas. He was in that role when I joined in 1990, and he led the group through some tremendous growth.

Even though Gene had no role in the Enron work as the Houston OMP, he had to be the one to go to court and testify on behalf of the firm. I learned this when I saw him walking into the Houston courthouse covered by CNN on national television. What an incredible act of selfless service. The courage it must have taken to do that is incredible. I admire this man for humbling himself and doing what he could to help represent the people and the firm he loved. He was one of the good guys.

Years before, he had shown me his character when I had switched into consulting from auditing. A project had gone south and we had a $200,000 write off. My partner on the project had left the office to take a job elsewhere in the firm and our project had been cancelled by our client due to his absence. I was a new manager on the project and was the one left to take the fall in Charlotte. In my seven years with the firm I'd never had to take a write off, let alone one this large and unexpected. Protocol designated that without a partner to take the write off, the manager had to fill out the form, detailing the loss and hand-deliver it for review with the OMP.

I was incredibly nervous about taking this to Gene, but I knew it had to be done. I was terrified of what his reaction would be and what this would mean for my career. I walked into his corner office, which was intimidatingly large—about the size of four partners' offices. He was seated behind his large desk and I sat down in front of him. He looked up with a smile and said, "What can I do for you, Mike?"

I told him about the write off and what had happened and the $200,000 loss. I saw his face turning red as I finished. He was clearly getting angry and upset, and I waited for what I thought was sure to be a verbal beating and maybe even dismissal.

Gene quickly calmed down before saying anything, regained his composure, and his face went back to its normal color. Then he said, "Mike, this is not your fault. I know the details of this project already. I know you did your best. This will not affect your standing with me or with this firm. I want to make sure you understand that."

I was overwhelmed by his response. The financial loss was obviously something that would affect his office and performance. Despite that fact he did the right thing. And even though he was upset he found a way to act with the utmost integrity.

Many of these situations became the background for the values and culture of Independence Consulting as Terry and I worked through the process that day in July. Rewriting and whittling them down for clarity took several hours. These values were published on our website.

Make an impact

- Provide clients a high return for fees paid
- Create financial success and stability for our clients and our people
- Invest in the personal and professional development of our clients and our people

Do the right thing

- Do the right thing in every situation–no matter the cost
- Put ourselves in our clients' and teammates' shoes with each decision we make
- Invest in sustainable charities

Love where you work

- Foster a fun, inspiring, and team-oriented environment
- Encourage initiative and creativity in problem solving
- Seek balance and quality of life for our people and their families

At about 3:30 that afternoon, after my car wreck that morning, I must have looked terrible, because Terry said, "Mike, I'm going to make you stop working now. You need to go home and get some rest."

Yes, I did need rest. Once I got home I realized that I had had a concussion, thank heaven not a serious one, so I was able to continue business planning.

Now it's your turn. As you enter a new company or get a new job within your current company, think about your past jobs.

What might you want to emulate? Mention that here:

____

____

____

____

What could you improve upon? Write that below:

____

____

____

____

Making these changes might not be easy, but don't get discouraged. Get fired up! Just keep on, keeping on.

CHAPTER 12

Step Ten: Keep Your Options Open

Network with People You Trust

Because the non-solicit agreement I signed with North Highland prohibited me from working with my former clients for two years I would have to start completely over with new relationships. For that reason, Kelli and I decided we might as well open the office in our town of Davidson, rather than in uptown Charlotte near my former big-bank clients. At this time I also had to find office space.

Over that next week I found the only Class A office space that was available in Davidson at the Flatiron Building on Main Street. The building is a mini, three-story version of the Flatiron Building in New York City. I loved the location as it was only three-hundred yards from our rented home. How cool would it be to walk to work?

We stayed in the rental house for that year until December when we decided to build a house. This time I was patient— leading from behind as I had been taught— because I knew the only thing that brought a smile to Kelli's face was the thought of building. She'd never really felt great about moving into someone else's house. I really thought we needed to be settled sooner so I showed her more than twenty houses. Even though my natural push to do things quickly was still there, I was able to keep it at bay and be in tune with what Kelli wanted. It would take us more than a year to build, but it would be a joy to watch our home come to life from the ground up. Being patient, renting, and building was the best real-estate decision we've ever made.

The office space that was available was on the third floor of this three-story building. We got off the elevator and the landlord opened the door to the space. I walked through the clean, newly renovated lobby and around the corner into a large, open-plan work area, which was flooded with light from big glass windows. The space was empty of furniture, but the tile flooring on the foyer and entry area, the carpet on the main area, and the furnishings all looked brand new and clean. It had been previously occupied by a design firm that had good taste.

At that moment, standing in this beautiful new office, it was as if the pilot light was relit inside of me and I felt the fire in my belly return. I wanted to build something special right here in this space. I thought to myself, *I'm not sure what kind of consulting business this is going to end up being, but I do know that I am excited to get up in the morning and come to work here.*

I had prayed to God to give me the inspiration and he supplied, in his way, in his timing. My experience has been that when God calls you to do something big, he will give you the time, the energy, the money, and whatever you need to fulfill his calling. It may not come in the way or the timing you expect *but* he will provide.

The next day I asked our commercial real-estate agent to try to talk the building folks down from demanding a five-year lease. I was not comfortable with anything more than two years. I said a prayer about it and gave it to God so that I could focus on a trip I had planned for just Olivia and me to Disney World. We were both happy to be getting away.

Those three days were so relaxing and fun. Having the time to put 100 percent of my focus into Olivia was pure joy. We both felt like little kids again. As we boarded the plane for the trip home, I received a text from my real-estate agent. "Mike, give me a call when you can. I have an interesting development on the office space."

I called him right back out of curiosity and learned that the owners came back and said we could have the space for one year for a little less than they had originally asked per-square foot and much less than the original five-year duration.

Thank you, Father, I thought. Miraculously we had been given more than what we hoped for on the lease. We had a fun, convenient, beautiful place to work for the next year.

Kelli, Olivia, and I designed the space and ordered furniture. We knew we wanted to make the large open space in the middle of the office very flexible. We envisioned doing creative thinking and strategy facilitation with clients in this large, open area. For the first four months, I was the only one in this space, which was large enough for a team of twenty. We moved in late August and made due, working on a folding table Kelli's dad had given us, which he used to filet the fish he caught on the lake. I used my son's Yeti cooler as my seat until our furniture arrived. By late August the desks were being installed.

On Monday, August 31, 2015, just minutes after they finished installing my desk, my cell phone rang. It was my neighbor from Atlanta, Harsha Agadi, the former COO of Domino's Pizza, former CEO of Church's Chicken, and former CEO of Krystal Burger. He and I had become good friends during my time in Atlanta. He had taken care of me when I was sick with bronchitis, making sure I had access to the best doctors. He had also offered to try to get me a position on the Board of Directors of Crawford and Company in Atlanta. We never got around to making that happen, but we had stayed in touch.

Harsha said, "Mike, how are you doing, sir? I've just been named the interim CEO of Crawford. Would you be interested in being considered for the CEO role permanently?"

Without thinking about how lucky I was to be getting the call, I laughed out loud and said, "Harsha, you know I can't move back to Atlanta. We just got back to North Carolina."

"I thought you might say that Mike, knowing how important your family is to you. How about you come and help me with a project then?

At that moment I didn't realize fully what was happening. Exactly what Jesus had spoken to Kelli was coming true: "Your friends are going to call you and you need to be prepared."

A few hours later I was on the phone with Harsha and the chairman of Crawford's Board. They wanted me to come in for six weeks and help them reorganize the company and save over $30 million. It sounded like incredibly hard work for a first assignment.

The next week I went to Atlanta to meet with Harsha and brought Kelli along with me. She was gung-ho about me getting started on the work. I was not feeling up for it at all. I was still letting fear grip me. How can I deliver a global reorganization and find that much savings in such a short period? Kelli's wise and straight-forward advice was this, "Mike, your friend needs your help and his company needs someone like you with integrity. You need to help your friend."

It was during this period of uncertainty that Terry Lursen texted me "out of the blue" with these words: "Keep your options open." Even with this kind of non-coincidental direction from God I was still reluctant.

The evening after my meeting with Harsha, I fell asleep in the hotel room with Kelli by my side. I went to bed feeling anxious and not ready to tackle this challenge. At 4:00 A.M. I woke up and sat straight up, having heard from God in my sleep. *Breathe life into that company, Michael.*

I got up quickly, dressed, grabbed my computer, and went downstairs into the lobby area where I wrote our first proposal in four hours. By the time Kelli woke up at 8:00 A.M. I had finished the proposal and scheduled a lunch with Harsha before we headed back to Charlotte.

Even though I'd tried to shoot myself in the foot, a week later we started our first engagement with Crawford, which launched Independence Consulting and enabled us to be profitable in our first half-year of operation. We finished the work in time for their board meeting. Along with their top management team we helped identify $30 million in savings, which lifted the equity value of the company by $150 million when the savings were reflected in their results in the first half of 2016. Our fees were a small fraction of that, and the company ended up with more than a one-hundred times return on their one-time investment in us. Since then they have adopted all our organizational recommendations and have a stronger management team now because of it.

I realized later that even though cost-takeout work, which can involve job loss for some and job change for others, is hard, someone needs to do it and it might as well be a company that has the long-term, best interests of the client in mind. We were off to a fast start, albeit ironically back in Atlanta for me. We were incredibly thankful to have a new calling, to be clear on God's purpose for our lives, and to be off and running in it.

When you feel you need to change jobs or your current occupation, you should be intentional and selective about seeking out jobs and roles that fulfill your Life Purpose and Role Success Statements.

One of the biggest risks to anyone in transition is not with finding something—it is with accepting something too early that is off purpose. When you are in transition for any reason—you resigned, you are ready to make a change, you were fired or transitioned out—it is very important to step back and describe what you are looking for. What is your purpose and what are your definitions of success in your key roles as a human being? These descriptions represent your requirements. That way when a new opportunity does arise you have something to evaluate it against. Without this intentional work you are at risk of taking the next thing that comes your way and missing the opportunity of a lifetime: you risk not fulfilling your *true* God-given purpose.

Here is another way to think about it. If an opportunity comes your way and you haven't described what you are looking for, you are making a binary decision—yes or no. Instead you should be scoring it against the requirements defined in your Life Purpose and Role Success Statements. Making sure you define what you are looking for before you are in a pressure, yes/no situation is so important to ensure your next assignment is *on purpose*.

Have integrity about only doing things that are aligned. Score out new opportunities against what you wrote in Chapter Eight as your Life Purpose and Role Success Statements. Right now go through Step Six— Analyze Where You Are and complete the Current Situation and New Opportunity Scoring System below—again.

Current Situation and New Opportunity Scoring System

Evaluation against Your "Requirements"

1. Think about your Life Purpose Statement and the key elements contained in it. For each element give yourself a score from 1—My current job/situation completely inhibits me from living out this aspect of my purpose—to 10—My current job/situation fully enables me to live out this aspect of my purpose.
2. For each of your Role Success Statements give yourself a similar score from 1—My current job/situation completely inhibits me from fulfilling this Role Success Statement—to 10—My current job/situation fully enables me to fulfill this Role Success Statement.

Wait on God to give you your calling. Immerse yourself in the Bible. Pray hard. Be intentional about networking with people you trust and respect to gain perspective. Pray that God will lead the right people into your path and keep away those who would distract you from finding his path for you.

CHAPTER 13

Step Eleven: Take an Annual Review Each Year

A Suggested Annual Review Process

From our company's birth on July 5, 2015, we got off to a fast start, thanks to the work we were doing in Atlanta. We were very blessed to have a great client, but we were also very focused on getting into new companies in the Charlotte market, near our office and home in Davidson, North Carolina. As a startup we knew sacrifices, like periodic full-time travel, would be required. This was especially important in the period I was subject to a non-solicit, which prohibited me from working with every large company in Charlotte. We did well that year to break even by putting together a string of mid-size companies in the Carolinas that were new clients.

While we waited out the non-solicit, I was intentional about targeting the only large bank in the state that I had never worked with. In the fall of 2016, after a yearlong effort, we were successful in getting a good-size project with this top-twenty-five, financial-services company. It was an exciting and high-impact project.

That Christmas we had completed the work and the client was very happy, saying, "We don't work well with most consultants; however, this project was the best executed piece of work we have seen in a long time." The project had gone so well that the CEO and CIO asked me if I'd be interested in coming onboard full-time. This was a great compliment, but we'd hired four people by this time, and I felt sure I was supposed to keep working on growing and sustaining Independence Consulting. That first project led the bank to ask us to assist them with a second project to implement the recommendations we had developed.

At the same time Harsha called again and needed help with another very important and high impact assignment. I've used the analogy of "the puppy that caught the bus" to describe what it is like when you land a huge project that is so big you struggle to figure out how you are going to deliver it. Neither project was so big or difficult on its own, but with only four people it was like the puppy chasing and catching two buses! I felt very fortunate, but also a little overwhelmed, since the deadline for both projects was in the same two-week period.

Thankfully I had just hired my best friend Keith Anthony whom I had worked with for twelve years, and he was a financial-services guru. Keith was the first person I had hired at North Highland and together, with a very talented team of consultants, we had grown an $80-million, financial-services practice. He had left North Highland and taken the summer off with his kids while he contemplated what he wanted to do next.

In September of 2016 he called and said, "Mike, I have been enjoying the time off with the kids this summer, but now they are back in school. I've done every honey-do list item Karen could think of for me. I'm ready to jump back in. I'm looking at other options, but wanted to see if you had any interest."

After a quick consult with my attorney we got the green light, since we had not recruited Keith while he was still at North Highland.

This was extremely happy news for Kelli and me. Keith and Karen and Kelli and I had known each other twelve years. We had literally watched our kids grow up, had built a big part of North Highland together, and had enjoyed the whole ride, bumps and all. One of these bumps on the periphery of our work was as dramatic as they come. You see, Keith and I were working together on January 15, 2009, when on a trip back from New York City he had been on the plane with 155 other passengers who made the miracle landing on the Hudson River.

That day I had gotten the call that the plane went down, had confirmed that he was on it, yet I did not know the plane was floating. It was the longest minute of my life. I knew the statistics and it was highly unlikely anyone would survive.

As we mobilized a command center from North Highland's offices in Atlanta and New York my iPhone rang. "Keith Anthony" flashed on my screen. I still get goose bumps thinking about that moment. It was like a ghost was calling me....

"Hello," I said with a lump in my throat.

"Mike, it's Keith. I'm standing on the shore of the Hudson River. I've already talked to Karen to let her know I'm fine. They are putting us on a bus now, so I won't be able to talk but I can text."

"Okay, buddy, thank God! We have people going over to be with Karen, and we will work on making arrangements to get you home."

So, I guess you could say that even though starting a company can be scary, risky, and a ton of hard work, at times it does not compare to how scary that day was. This harrowing accident helps put things in their proper perspective, and when we really think about it this experience ensures we are thankful for each and every day we get to take a breath and do this.

Now in the fall of 2016, Keith and I decided to divide and conquer the two big projects—the North Carolina bank and Harsha's second project—and we were off and running. It was the most profitable and busiest couple of months I'd had. Both clients wanted me heavily involved so I was literally trying to be in two states at once. Although these projects were both individually challenging, they were very doable given our backgrounds; however, with such a small, four-person team and the requirement for me to be heads down on the delivery for each project it was taxing mentally and physically. With the perspective of hindsight, I wonder if I should have said "No" to one of them? That would be a seemingly crazy decision at the time for a young fledgling business. My gut told me I was trying to take on too much, but my head was telling me to figure out how to serve both client's needs. In order to grow further we needed to serve both. Growth is hard at times. You need to push and stretch yourself. However, I've learned the hard way that you need to also recognize your limits and be smart about how you grow.

On February 23, 2017, I was feeling pretty good about our projects and the company. We had successfully completed Harsha's project and we were cranking away hard on the final deliverable for the second project. The week we were to deliver the final presentation to the big bank was a stressful time, since we had to quickly synthesize four weeks of work into a cohesive game plan for the company. This is both a creative and analytical process and we did it together as a team.

As we reached the finish line and were printing out the final document, I thought it was time to have a little fun. I pulled over the large, grey yoga ball that is supposed to be used for sitting. I started bouncing on it, and as I gained confidence I bounced higher and higher. I got so good at it I asked my business partner Keith to film a Snapchat for my kids.

The first time I did it I executed the bounces and dismount onto our office bean bag perfectly. The second time didn't work out so well. As I bounced higher and just before the launch to the bean bag, I hit the ball a bit off center. Instead of flying into the bean bag I fell backwards, landing on my butt first, but then on my back and my neck—and finally on my head, which whiplashed straight down onto the floor, where only a thin layer of commercial carpet covered the concrete.

Our office manager, Anne Banez, heard the sound from inside her office with the door closed. It made a terrible thud. How could something so silly turn into something so serious this fast? From that moment forward for about two months I wasn't myself and didn't realize the gravity of the situation. I would later learn that I could have died or have been permanently brain damaged from the accident.

Immediately after it happened I was shaken up for a second, like football players when they have their bell rung. Keith told me later that for a split second I was jumbling my words, but then I seemed okay. I went into my office and did a call for about forty-five minutes with an executive from that large bank that we were just completing their deliverable. Other than a mild headache I was still feeling okay. I finished my call and walked back into our main area to see the team. Keith asked me something about the guy I had just talked to. I couldn't remember his name! And my words were jumbled. Keith said, "We need to call Kelli and take you to a doctor." The last thing I can remember is sitting on the sidewalk, up against the wall of our building, balled up and holding my hands on the top of my head.

The moment Kelli arrived she and Keith jumped into action, getting me quickly to the nearest hospital. I don't remember any of this. They did a CAT scan and immediately realized my brain had swollen so much that they needed to send me to Carolinas Medical Center where they were equipped to do the surgery necessary to relieve the swelling if it got worse. My poor, sweet wife was scared to death. After losing her dad a few years ago she was now facing the loss of her husband.

For a long time, I thought that I had gone airborne that day and landed on the top of my head, because the top of my head felt bruised. What I would learn weeks later from watching the video of the accident and from the CAT scans is that I hit the floor with the back of my head. This caused my brain to ricochet around inside my skull.

First my brain hit the back, but then rebounded to move twice the distance to hit the front of my skull. My brain bled from the impact on the front of the skull, leaving a bloody area that was about the size of my thumb, directly behind my eyes. The CAT scans also revealed that my brain had swollen so much that the ridges you would normally see on an image of the top of the brain were not visible. My brain was pressed flat against the top of my skull!

After a night and day of touch-and-go reports from the doctors as to whether they would need to do surgery to relieve the pressure, the swelling finally subsided. I had four days in the hospital, and I only have faint memories of the last day when they let me leave. Those first three days were very tough on Kelli. She knew how serious the injury was, but she didn't want to scare her mom, our kids, our friends, and our co-workers. My good friend Mike Sefryn kept trying to visit and I would say, "No," but he did check in with Kelli and he and his wife, Jen, were praying for us. My former trainer and friend Terry Lursen kept texting as well; for some reason I told Kelli he could come. I barely remember seeing his white hair as he stood over my bed. Terry's presence meant a tremendous amount to Kelli as she had felt so alone and scared. Kelli was by my side for those four long days. Praying and worrying.

Amid something so scary, something funny unfolded. I don't remember this so I'm taking Kelli's word for it (smiley face)! Apparently, I said and did a lot of weird stuff while my brain was swollen, and the brain bleed was happening. The most notable story was from my second night in the hospital. From the time I checked in, I would not let them put the hospital gown on me. I don't know if it was because I thought the gown was ugly, which I had always thought, or uncomfortable, but I would not wear it. I was comfortable in nothing but my "tighty whities."

What a sight for that poor hospital staff! A 230-pound (maybe 240-pound) chubby baby! From this point on I would like for you to refer to me as Captain Underpants! Well, apparently one night I decided I'd had it; I was going to check myself out and go home. I got out of bed in my underpants and told Kelli I was leaving. She tried to talk me out of it, and I just gently moved her to the side. She begged me to put on some clothes. I guess I sort of complied, because I took the bed sheet and tied it around my neck like a Superman cape. Up, up, and away Captain Underpants!

It took three security guards to stop Captain Underpants from getting out the front door. They tranquilized me—like a wild animal. Imagine the hospital police tasering Captain Underpants or better yet, tranquilizing him with a blow dart like an elephant in the wild. Captain Underpants was then literally strapped to the bed for the next two days. Thankfully I don't remember that either. I never have liked to sit still!

A traumatic brain injury is a serious matter. I'd never experienced anything like it. As I said I don't remember three full days. Day four I remember glimpses: Terry visiting, going to the bathroom, climbing into my bed at home. For two solid weeks I slept most of the day and night and only got up to eat and use the bathroom. During week two I went to therapy and evaluation. They did motor tests to see if my brain function was improving. By the end of week two I started to feel like myself again, at least mentally. I vividly remember having a thought about God and realizing that for two straight weeks I hadn't had a thought like that. I love my relationship with God and it is something I think about and rely on all day long. It was so strange that I didn't have this direction or didn't even realize that it hadn't been there during the prior two weeks.

I was told that the recovery process would be six-to-eight weeks, which is exactly how it unfolded. Two weeks at home in bed was how it started. During the third week the doctor cleared us to go on our planned vacation to the Grand Cayman. She said I couldn't hurt myself but to just rest anytime I felt fatigued.

I remember everything from that trip. It was great for my family to get away and relax. I could only do about twenty-to-thirty minutes on the beach, because of the heat and sun so I watched virtually every NCAA basketball game as part of March Madness. As my mind started to come back I can now remember that is when the anxiety started creeping in. Would I make a full recovery? How much work would I miss? Would my business recover from the lack of sales during my absence? How would my missing work affect us financially? Would I be able to get new work with our other clients?

It was hard to cope with these questions/doubts on top of not feeling 100 percent. Without realizing it, my circumstances were mentally knocking me off my game. God had called me to start this company. Why wasn't it going better? Later I would reflect on this. God doesn't call us to do something and promise it is going to be easy. My experience is that nothing truly good comes easily.

After three weeks I returned to work with approval from the doctor. Her only instruction was when you feel fatigued, go home and take a rest. The fourth week I was feeling better, and I was able to work for three-to-four hours at a time without having fatigue. When I felt exhausted, I would stop and go home and rest. From week five to eight I was able to go longer without taking a break until week eight when I was able to go the whole week without resting.

Once I was fully healed and my mind was sharp, I realized just how serious my injuries were, and I had an overwhelming feeling of thankfulness. Thankful that I was alive and that I'd made a full mental recovery from the accident. Many people had prayed for my healing and recovery while I was in the hospital. Kelli had prayed extensively, crying out to God on our behalf. When people ask if I have any lingering effects I joke, "I'm only as good as I used to be. I didn't pick up any special powers." I wish I could carry that extreme feeling of thankfulness every day for the rest of my life, but it is easy to get caught up in the next struggle, which was going to be how we could regroup and rebuild our client base and our company from scratch.

From April to July of 2017 we decided to set a new strategy to focus on the biggest companies in Charlotte and Atlanta, those that could sustain a healthy consulting business. It would take time to get back into these places once my non-solicit agreement expired in late July. It would be another big investment of time and some money, but it felt like the way we needed to go for the long-term success of the business. We made the decision to find an uptown Charlotte location to be near the big clients and allow us to hire people from all over Charlotte. It took us six months to plan our strategy, determine the first 100 individual clients we would focus on, rebrand our company, and launch a new website.

On October 17 we moved into our new location. We spent over $100,000 designing and building our new office on the thirtieth floor of an uptown skyscraper in the center of Charlotte at Trade and Tryon streets. Because it takes four-to-six months to get into these big companies, we knew there would be an investment period where we would be draining cash. From August 1 to October 11, 2017 I met with the 100 clients we had selected. In early October we were awarded a piece of work at one of the top five, financial-services firms in the country, which was approved by their CEO, and along with it they decided to add us to their Global Preferred Consulting Program. It was great news, but it wouldn't be until November 1 before we would see our first cash in the door since March.

During the "dry spell" from March to November of 2017, we had to make some difficult financial decisions to stay the course. We needed to generate cash to fund our family obligations with two kids in college and our youngest in private school. We sold one of our cars, and we dipped deeper into our savings to bridge the gap. It was another gut-check moment that tested mine and Kelli's priorities. We loved what we were doing, we loved the calling we had received, and we were willing to do what was necessary to fulfill it. We had tremendous passion for our company, the values we were committed to uphold, the importance of the work we did for clients and the way we did it.

Yet we have learned to be careful about being overcommitted. God called us to start Independence Consulting, but he did not tell us to kill ourselves trying to "make it happen." We would continue to do this if we knew it was a good thing for our family, our people, and our clients. Through the dry spell we were always transparent with our team and each other about what needed to happen to keep going. We shared our cash balance and all our financials monthly with the team. I thought it was important for them to know the reality of starting a business. It is not easy, and it involves uncertainty and a tremendous amount of hustle. The ups and downs can feel extreme when business is this personal. The crazy thing is though, I love it. It is thrilling to see so tangibly the results of our hard work.

My main reason for sharing all the gory details is this. I don't want anyone to think that following your God-given purpose is all smooth sailing. It is going to involve hills and valleys. You will experience setbacks. Through it all, though, I would encourage you to keep trying to move forward. It is all about taking more steps forward than backward.

Each summer since we started the company, Kelli and I have done an Annual Review. It is a process we use to assess how we are doing against our Life Purpose and Role Success Statements. It is invaluable to making course corrections or improvements. Most years this isn't a dramatic change, but it results in key strategic actions that we feel move us closer to our purpose. Think of it like a pivot in basketball or tacking and gybing in sailing. This is part of being a life-long learner. It is critical to be humble and ask, "What could I be doing better? What specific adjustments can I make to improve my performance and move closer to or better in line with my purpose?"

That summer in 2017 when I was recovering, we did the assessment described in this chapter. We decided we would give it our best for the balance of the year. We set in motion 100 intentional meetings with clients that I'm happy to report ended with two, very-strategic new clients that we are still working with today. One is a top-five bank and the other is a top institution of higher learning. We will not boast about tomorrow. We are thankful for the clients and colleagues we have today. We thank God for his provision and for his calling.

One of the false teachings prevalent in the faith community is that when you accept Christ or when you are living in his will, everything will lead to material prosperity. There have been times in my life where I have seen this to be partially true. When I've been living according to my God-given purpose and working very hard to see things through, I have experienced periods of significant material gain.

However, I have also had periods where my material possessions shrunk. Yet eternal victories were flourishing with my family and with people coming to know Jesus through the work and missions we were a part of. Do not mistake living out God's purpose for you as taking the easy or financially successful road.

God's purpose for your life will be challenging.

God's purpose for your life will test your faith.

However, your life will have new meaning, and it will produce dividends with perseverance and faith in God. My Grandfather Alvin T.M. Lee used to say, "Nothing good ever comes easy," and I believe this is true. It can be much more satisfying when you accomplish big things for God if it involves hard work and sacrifices—and even tests along the way.

Dealing with Unexpected Tests

Now that you have your Life Purpose Statement—your God-given purpose defined—you are ready for a sailing adventure. However, before you get started, I want to warn you. The enemy will try to knock you off track, even before you pull your ropes off the dock. Satan is the author of confusion and the father of all lies. Watch out! Be vigilant! You might even be tested by God.

Not long after God called Kelli and I to start Independence Consulting I mentioned Harsha calling me with a CEO opportunity. And a week before Harsha called, I had gotten a call from another acquaintance who knew the chairman of the board of a large media company, looking for a new CEO.

Again, this was a friend I knew well through board connections. He said, "Mike, would you be interested in this role?"

I explained that we were committed to the family staying in Davidson, but that I really appreciated the thought.

"Do you want to know the pay package?" he asked.

"No, thank you, my friend."

He told me anyway, saying, "It is two-to-three million dollars."

"I told you not to tell me…." We both laughed, and I politely declined.

I believe this was a test, which God allowed, to see if I had learned anything. Would I place his instructions and the needs of my family over a large compensation package and the CEO title I almost had? I have to admit that even though this was an attractive offer, it was a very easy decision, because I had written my purpose and defined my priorities before the call came in.

There have been times since we started the company where a steady monthly pay seemed very attractive; however, we wouldn't trade living our purpose and his calling for anything.

You see, living in your God-given purpose means using it to filter the things you say yes to and those you need to say no to. This God-given purpose helps prioritize many seemingly positive courses you could take so you can stay focused on the path God has created you for. That means saying no to projects, causes, people, and distractions that keep you from the most important things.

Take a moment to think about the path you are on now and prioritize the choices you
Will say yes to:

____

____

Will say no to:

____

____

Now let's look in more depth to what is involved with an annual review process.

Annual Review Process

Once you have clarity on your God-given purpose there are two key components of Step Nine: An Annual Review. Keep your Life Purpose Statement and Role Success Statements somewhere you can see them. Display them in your office or home so you will stay focused on the things that are most important. I also want to emphasize important regular routines: stay in the Word, develop a strong prayer life, and find a great church family and network that can support you in your spiritual and physical journey in this life.

When you feel off kilter or a little lost, you can always fall back on my favorite Scripture: Micah 6:8 says, "And what does the Lord require of you but to do justly, to love mercy, and to walk humbly with your God?"[7] I believe this is a complete job description for our life, provided by God himself. When you feel lost just do that! Please keep in mind that this process does not mean you need to change jobs or even your situation. Most times in our lives we go through periods of difficulty to teach us something—and to grow. If we quit too soon, we may miss out on something we are supposed to learn. It is a difficult process to go through and discern what to do. Lean on God in these situations. Talk with him, and more importantly listen to him, through Scripture reading, prayer time, finding a trainer, and putting yourself around good solid people at church and in the community. Scripture says it best…

"In all your ways acknowledge Him, and He shall direct your paths."[8]

And every year follow this straightforward process to evaluate how you are doing against your Life Purpose Statement and Role Success Statements. Give yourself a score of 1 (needs serious improvement) and 5 (I'm doing great in this area).

Make a promise to yourself to make these changes happen in the next week. Write them down and share them with your spouse, significant other, friend, or trainer.

Below I've given you an example of what I did at that time in my life.

1. Needs serious improvement. 5. I'm doing great in this area.

Life Area	Score	Promises
I am living out my purpose in my daily life.	3 - I am currently burdened by the weight of having to sell work with a small team and deliver the work once sold to survive. I followed God's calling to start the business, which is great, but I need to be open to changes in direction to survive or improve.	I will be open to alternative ways to sustain the company, our clients, and our people. I will not be stubborn and hold onto our current setup. I will apply what I learned during my North Highland transition and not feel stuck or frozen by fear.
I am spending my time on things that fulfill my purpose.	3 - I am spending nearly all of my time on sales and delivery of work and do not have as much time to develop people.	I will look for opportunities to grow our company so we can work with more people and increase the impact we have on the world.
I am spending time with people who are enabling God's purpose in my life.	3 - I've been so focused on work I've not been spending time with my family, my friends, and a trainer who might have valuable insights.	I will spend more time with my family. I will look for a new trainer and make a list of my friends and contacts whom I can trust for great advice and wisdom.
I feel close to God and am immersed in his Word.	3 - I've drifted away from my morning Bible reading and prayer time. I'm still doing my Bible study on Fridays, but that is all.	It is time to reinstitute my daily Bible reading. I will read a Proverb and a Psalm each morning and study favorite passages that relate to my circumstances.

I feel focused on what is most important.	4 - I do feel focused on sales for the business, which I believe is the most important thing, but maybe I need help.	I will open my mind to finding other companies or partners that might be able to help us grow.
I am caught up in unhealthy habits.	1 - As the stress level has risen I have exercised less.	I will start exercising each morning with a group of men as a way to get healthy and also develop relationships.

Now it is your turn! Be candid with where you are right now and be specific on what you need to improve. Then look back at the lowest scores and write down what you are going to do in this area to make improvement in the Promises column.

1. Needs serious improvement. 5. I'm doing great in this area.

Life Area	Score	Promises
I am living out my purpose in my daily life.		
I am spending my time on things that fulfill my purpose.		

I am spending time with people who are enabling God's purpose in my life.		
I feel close to God and am immersed in his Word.		
I feel focused on what is most important		
I am caught up in unhealthy habits		

Now take out your Role Success Statements for the five most important people in your life. Let's limit it to five here. Give yourself the same 1 to 5 rating on how you are performing against your role statements and then write what you might do in the future in the Promises column:

1. Needs serious improvement. 5. I'm doing great in this area.

Role Success Sentence	**Score**	**Promises**
EXAMPLE: Cami's Father – I want her to say that I was present in her life and that when I was with her I was focused on her. I want her to know that I love her and that I'm available for her.	4 - I listened when she asked to return to Charlotte.	In the next year I'm going to make a point to share an inspiring or calming Scripture with her daily.
Your Role 1		
Your Role 2		
Your Role 3		

Your Role 4		
Your Role 5		
Your Role 6		
Your Role 7		

Inevitably you will find yourself struggling again. There are times in this fallen world where tough things happen that require us to reevaluate everything. Even in situations where God has called you to something new, you need to be aware and open to a change in direction.

Part Three

My Next Chapter and Your Next Chapter

CHAPTER 14

From Point A to Point B

A Change in Direction

From our Annual Review in the summer of 2018 to January of 2019, Kelli and I tried to determine the course of Independence Consulting in the next ten-to-fifteen years. We strategized and planned how we could grow our company to help more clients and create a great work environment for more people. Our company culture—truly caring for our clients and our people—and our values—always seeking to do the right thing—are so important to us. So is our ability to give back 10-20 percent of our net income to sustainable charities.

We had grown from just me and Kelli, part-time, to a small, but tight and experienced, team of eight. Keith and I bore the majority of the burden for selling business, and our whole team was involved in delivery of the work we generated. When you compare eight people to the thousand we had been a part of before, it put us at a disadvantage when calling on very large companies. We had done well to land six clients, but we were constantly caught in the chicken-and-egg cycle of having to sell the work before we could hire the new person who would be needed to fulfill it. We were interested in hiring more people ahead of any demand to grow faster. That required more capital.

We explored many options for staying independent and maintaining ownership and control of the company so that we could do these things. We looked to raise capital to enable growth, and we opened many doors from bank loans to raising private equity to fuel our growth.

We soon realized that an inherent problem with bank loans is that banks only want to loan you a lot of money when you are generating high and consistently positive cash flows. That is not the nature of a young consulting firm with the ups-and-downs in client business. One quarter you are flying high with more work than you know what to do with, and another quarter you have no work and are hustling to land the next deal. The other issue is banks do not really understand professional-services companies. They like to loan against hard assets. In consulting all you have are your people and their minds. A unique, valuable combination, but not hard assets like inventory or facilities you can touch and put a value on.

We also fully vetted the private-equity route. We networked to find competent people whom we knew we could trust and who were focused on building sustainably healthy companies. It is possible we just didn't meet the right people, but the ones we met with told us that for this model to work, we had to be willing to give up control of our company. Yet change in control might compromise the way we serve our clients, treat our people, and invest in our community. Our main reason for existing as

Independence Consulting was to foster a special culture and a firm set of values—mainly in "doing the right thing" in all that we do. We were not willing to potentially compromise on this by bringing in outside investors who justifiably expect their #1 focus to be on driving high returns on their money.

Please understand I also want to drive long-term financial returns for our shareholders and employees. My hypothesis is that if you focus on your clients and your people, you will create the long-term value for shareholders. If you focus on financial returns primarily at the expense of your clients and your people, you will ultimately destroy long-term, shareholder value. We could not feel comfortable that the private-equity route would allow us to protect and nurture our culture and values.

None of those doors felt right, based on our detailed analyses, financial-scenario plans, and our gut feeling.

As I struggled with these questions, I kept going back to my Annual Review in 2017 and my Life Purpose Statement and my Role Success Statements. I had said I was spending nearly all of my time on sales and delivery of work and did not have much time to develop people. I'd not been spending as much time with my family and hadn't been spending time with friends and a trainer. I was not fulfilling my desire to be really present with my family. Our youngest, Olivia, would only be home for two more years, and I didn't want to look back, regretting that I hadn't spent enough quality time with her. I had drifted away from my morning Bible reading and prayer time. In the heat of the battle this Annual Review Process helped me remember what I was really trying to accomplish.

From my review against my priorities I also considered the questions, "How can we make the biggest impact in the world, both in business and in charitable causes? How can we serve more clients? How can we serve more colleagues?" Our motivation was to maximize impact for people. Finally, it was increasingly taxing to be doing this on our own. I didn't know it yet, but I was getting mentally prepared for the idea that we didn't have to do it all on our own. There might be other options.

I've learned that sometimes when you hit a wall, it forces you to think differently. You must be flexible enough to take a different route to accomplish God's purposes. Being stubborn and prideful is dangerous for you and your family. You can't get fixed on one way. How could we take a different path? Taking a direct step up the mountain wasn't working. Was there another way up that mountain by taking a different route?

Yet it is easy to say "don't get fixed on one way," but it can be hard to apply in our lives. Once I get an idea in my head of how something is supposed to work out, I can get extremely fixated on making it happen that way. You've seen examples of that in Chapter Nine where I suggested that you might recalibrate some areas of your lifestyle as I did with my tendency to be assertive and impatient. It is a very good thing to be obedient to following God's instructions or calling on our lives, but it is very important not to confuse his calling with our ideas of how it should materialize or evolve over time. This is why Jesus taught us to pray a prayer that I'm getting better at praying more often, *Father, your will be done. Not my will but your will be done.* I've also learned to pray more often for "the mind of Christ" to help me determine new paths and make tough decisions. I can tell you he has never steered me wrong when I've asked him, though it has often led to surprising paths and interesting outcomes. Not surprisingly, what he had planned for me was more beautiful and more fulfilling than what I could have imagined.

So we were really torn about what we should do throughout the fall and winter of 2018. On the one hand we loved the autonomy and flexibility to serve our clients in a way that was 100 percent consistent with our stated values. We also truly enjoyed the opportunity to build a special team of eight people who genuinely trusted, respected, and challenged each other. Finally, even though starting a business from scratch is extremely hard, it is incredibly rewarding to see the fruits of that labor. A thrill only another entrepreneur understands. I will always have respect for those who forge out on their own with little-or-no safety net. These people are pioneers who risk much to create new things.

Despite the amazing attributes of starting and owning Independence Consulting it had some major drawbacks as well. The stress and strain of risking your own resources and the responsibility you have to your employees to provide a sustainable living is significant. With Alex and Cami in college, Kelli and I also had a major responsibility to follow through on our commitment to educate our children to the best of our ability. We are both inactive CPA's who understand the financial requirements of the business. We routinely ran cash-flow projections that calculated how long we could survive, depending on different sales scenarios. Just like the work we do with our clients on scenario planning, we would run "best case" and "worst case" scenarios.

The bottom line was this: We loved what we were doing at Independence Consulting, but we needed more capital to continue and to grow our business. If we didn't hire more people, we weren't going to grow. After exhausting our options with banking partners and with private-equity firms, we were still scratching our heads. We didn't see a viable option forward so we prayed more as we continued to think hard about what we were missing. I was still fixated on how we could continue on our own by accessing capital—until the fire got hotter, and we were forced to be more creative in considering our options.

We needed to be open to a new direction.

One day, after many closed doors, I had a thought, *What if we sold our company to a group of like-minded professionals? People who have a passion for the same values and culture. People who believe in doing the right thing all the time and who genuinely care about their clients and their people. People who could share in the growth and in the struggles of building a company.* Then it hit me: There was only one company that I knew of from my twenty-eight years in consulting that fit that bill. A company founded in Seattle called Point B. *Fortune Magazine* rated them the #1 Best Mid-size Company to Work for in the United States.

I made a call to Mike Pongon, their CEO, whom I'd met seven years earlier when we were both presidents of our respective consulting firms. We had treated each other well at that time and stayed in touch. Point B had a several hundred-million-dollar business, primarily on the West Coast and Midwest with newer offices in Boston and New York, and our company had a great track record on the East Coast.

I said, "Mike, we've had a great run the last three-and a-half years, but I just want to run this idea past you. It seems to me that we are like two puzzle pieces, meant to fit together given your strength on the west coast and ours on the east coast. Most importantly I think we share the same culture and values. We have great qualifications in strategic planning, cost and efficiency improvement, and merger integration. I know you guys don't yet have an office in the southeast and that is where we have many relationships with clients and potential recruits from our twenty-nine years working in Charlotte and Atlanta primarily. We've also developed some deep technical expertise in the areas of Robotic Process Automation and Artificial Intelligence."

"I like the idea, Mike. Let me run it past my Board of Directors and Founders in two weeks and I'll be in touch."

For the next two weeks we stayed focused on growing our business, serving clients, and working on the banking and private-equity options. It was a busy and stressful time as we could not find a long-term, viable option. For now, we would stay focused on going it on our own and wait to hear back from Point B.

I knew the date of Point B's Board Meeting so when that day in November came and went with no news, I feared they were not interested; I knew Mike would call me if he had news. About a week after their board meeting, Mike Pongon called, "Hey Mike, we talked about it and we would like to explore doing something together. Could you and Keith Anthony meet me and a colleague in Atlanta in a few weeks?"

It didn't take me long to respond with, "Absolutely, Mike! We would enjoy that." Though I didn't realize it at the time the first step in their due-diligence process was for Mike to introduce us to a colleague Brian Anderson over dinner to see if we were a culture fit for them. The first measure of this was not complicated. Did we enjoy spending time together and could we see ourselves working together for years into the future?

We would end up meeting with over twenty-five people at Point B during the due-diligence process, including the entire Board of Directors, the leadership team, the operations leaders, and their Seattle and Chicago-based consultants. The company cares so much about their culture and values that they invest incredible amounts of time in ensuring there is a match with each business and leadership team they acquire. It took a lot of time on our part and theirs, which was stressful for me as we tried to also keep our business running. Still this signaled how seriously they took their culture and values. It was like I'd discovered a long-lost twin from whom I'd been separated at birth. We were made of the same DNA. Mike Pongon and I had the same first name. And now that we were in front of each other frequently he felt like a long-lost brother I had never met.

Being a part of Point B would open a whole new world of possibilities—new customers, new geographical areas, and new capabilities in strategy, venture capital, digital services, merger integration, and data and analytics. This deal would give my business partner Keith and I more assets that we could bring to bear for our clients, which would add maximum value for the client and help us be more successful against our larger competitors. Point B also extended our track record of delivering a variety of complex business and technology work for large and mid-size clients. They even have a business unit that focuses on helping customers with property development, which was unusual for a consulting company. I was excited to learn more about how this functioned. The best part, though, was the opportunity to connect with a new network of like-minded consulting colleagues.

At the end of a great trip to Seattle, their headquarters, to meet with their board and leadership team, Mike Pongon and I agreed that both parties would try to move forward quickly. We even thought we might have the acquisition of Independence Consulting into Point B completed before the end of the year. We were slightly optimistic on that front!

Five weeks later, in mid-January of 2019, I was still waiting to hear the final word on their approval for us to join their company. I have to admit I'd experienced anxiety about the deal. Would they say yes? What would we do if it didn't go through? Would we agree to financial terms that were mutually beneficial and agreeable?

I also experienced feelings of impatience. We had had to go through that due-diligence process on our company and our team, which had taken about five weeks. I had been impressed with the level of their detail and care when Ben Burke made a special trip to Charlotte to meet each member of our team one-on-one, to talk to our clients, and Dennin Brasch did a deep dive into our financials and our legal agreements. Dennin and Ben were great to work with, but they were also very thorough and detailed in their review. They had a job to do and they did it well. I always tried to put myself in their shoes to look at things from Point B's perspective. They genuinely cared about doing the right thing for the company and its employee owners.

Point B is 100 percent owned by its employees through an Employee Stock Ownership Plan (ESOP). What a cool model! As the company grows and does well, all employees are in it together. If the company experiences tough times, everyone shares in the burden of doing what is needed to survive. After the fog of due-diligence cleared, I realized how awesome it would be to have nine hundred and fifty colleagues across the United States with whom to collaborate and share the ups-and-downs of the business. I also realized that these were the type of people I wanted to go to battle with. They had great values, a strong culture, and I was learning they were very good at what they do.

Now that we were all ready and excited to join it was hard not to have a feeling of "let's get on with this." We could see the next chapter ahead of us, but we were not able to turn the page. We were stuck in the middle. Ready to launch out of the gates but held back for a period. Over the years I have learned the hard way that impatience is not always a good trait. It's good for getting consulting projects done on time, *but* sometimes you can push too hard and do harm.

As I thought about this I found a Scripture on Bible Gateway:

"Be still and know that I am God" (Psalm 46:10, NIV).

And just above the Scripture was a banner ad for guess who?

"Point B – World Class Business Consulting – Management Consulting and More"

I knew there might be a technical explanation for how my internet browser knew I was interested in Point B, since internet advertising allows ads to be brought up on your screen, based on previous searches you've done on Google, for example. Still I was going to take this as God's way of directly telling me to calm down, to be patient, to do the work I could, and to let him do the rest.

I clicked on this specific ad to see how Point B would advertise itself. . . .

Your Success. That's our Business.
We're management consultants.
We're property developers.
We're investors.
We're business leaders.
We're doers.
We're Point B.
We have big plans for you.

Their Point B website reads, "At Point B we envision, create and enact new opportunities to help our clients achieve their greatest potential. Whether you need to fix it, finance it, solve it, grow it or build it. Point B gets you there."

You've heard the phrase "We need to get from Point A to Point B." That is what the company does. They help clients envision a desired future state, and then they roll up their sleeves with their clients and enable them to get there. This was an epiphany moment for me. The work they do, and most importantly the way they do it, was a direct match for what I've spent my whole career doing and the work I have tremendous passion for continuing.

The interesting part of what I realized about the concept of Point A to Point B is that the saying works on two levels. First, at the corporate level, Point B enjoys helping companies determine a strategy and then successfully follow through, *but* second they also have a passion for helping their individual clients define their purpose and realize their full potential. At the individual level, whether it is a client or a friend, I have a passion for helping others find an amazing, purpose-driven life. As you know by now this book is all about articulating the requirements for what you want your life to be about and what gives your life meaning. I want to help every person I meet define their own unique Point B and help them get from Point A to Point B. The name, the logo, the people, and the values—everything about it felt right. This was an opportunity to help companies and individual people at the same time.

I was getting more excited about the seemingly incredible fit, but I was also anxious to see if the acquisition of our company by Point B would become reality.

I determined to have faith and trust God. No matter what.

Finally, on January 30, 2019, Keith and I had a scheduled call with Mike Pongon, Dennin Brasch, and Ben Burke to debrief the due-diligence. They made us an offer for our entire, full-time team to join Point B for the long term. Not wasting any time we called them back the next day to accept.

Point B planned on integrating us into their business and making us their new Charlotte office and growth executives, focused on East Coast expansion, financial-services customer growth, and on helping their firm increase relationships with the largest companies in the world. Although this route meant that Kelli and I would lose control of our business, I felt comfortable doing so, because we believe Point B is committed to the same culture and values that we had worked so hard to develop and nurture. We went from having eight colleagues to 950 overnight—all of whom share the same values: passion for life, purposeful professionalism, uncompromising ethics, accountability, and stewardship.

All our people, except Kelli, moved over to Point B, which was enjoyable as we saw the new opportunities this adventure brought to each of our folks. My wife did not come over as it would be unusual to have a husband and wife inside a division of their company, and they already have all the support services Kelli had been providing for us.

On a personal note Kelli and I had really enjoyed building the business together and even getting our children involved as interns as they were all high school and college-age then. Kelli handled all the finance, accounting, and human resources aspects, which allowed me to focus on client work and building our team. I miss the nightly quizzes she gave me, like "How is your sales pipeline right now? I want the details" to asking twenty-seven questions about my meetings that day. Not to mention how much I appreciate all she learned about consulting during those years, which came in handy when she had to run the company while I recovered from that brain injury for three months from March to June of 2017.

Kelli has been happy to consider taking time off to focus 100 percent on our family again. She had enjoyed the ownership experience, but was very ready to see me join a stable, well-run company, and get a steady paycheck again. One of the strangest things I've ever had to do was say to my wife and co-owner, "Kelli, you're fired!" We had a big laugh about that moment.

Consulting is not an easy business. You must constantly sell work to stay busy. It is challenging, but it is the business that I know and love.

Looking back with hindsight and perspective I've learned to accept, and even embrace, the periods of transition, frustration, and uncertainty. My experience has taught me that these "burning platform" moments are God's way of preparing me for what is next. I'm learning to trust him through the process. Submit to his will, not demand my will, for my life. I've learned to lean on him for peace, comfort, and direction when I'm in the valley and to praise him for the times he has provided a way forward and helped me ascend the next range of mountains in my life.

There have been times where Kelli and I have looked back and wondered, "What if we hadn't moved to Atlanta? What if we hadn't started Independence Consulting? Or what if I hadn't taken those two projects at once, gotten stressed out, jumped on the yoga ball, and injured myself?" It is easy to fall into the trap of looking back and wondering how things could have turned out differently. I believe in looking back on life's moments to see what you can learn and what you will take with you in your tool kit to help you or others in the future.

I feel equally strongly, though, that we are the people we are, not in-spite-of, but because of the mistakes we make, because of the chances we take, because of the challenges we overcome, and because of the difficulties we experience. I've learned to accept that I'm going to make mistakes. If we aren't willing to fail, we will not grow as we should. Now please understand I try not to repeat the same bonehead moves I've made in the past. We have removed the yoga balls from the office, for instance. I'm kidding, but not really kidding; they are long gone! What I am saying is we can't live our lives afraid of making mistakes. We can't live our lives looking backward, dreaming of "what might have been." We need to live our lives accepting and learning from our mistakes and levering them to do something important. We may even find that God can use our biggest failures to fulfill his purposes.

He can use the good, the bad, and even the ugly to do something wonderful. For instance, people who have experienced the terror of wanting to take their own lives have formed suicide-prevention charities. They have used their scars to help save others. So let's stop beating ourselves up. Stop second guessing. Let's change the conversation in our minds. Let's ask, "How can my experiences be used to help others?" Let's be honest with ourselves about what we did and move forward with confidence that it can be used for something incredible in the future. Let's believe what God says in his Word: "We know that all things work together for the good of those who love God, who are called according to His purpose."[9]

So, let's get out there and use our scars and experiences to do something important in this world. And let's be willing to seek advice from some who have walked this way before us.

Having lived through two start-ups, one with North Highland and one with Independence Consulting, I'm sometimes asked what advice I would give for those contemplating starting or having started a business. The first thing I would share is that I would not trade the experience for anything in the world. My experience with the growing pains, the successes and failures, have all shaped my approach to how we do business moving forward. It has given me perspectives that some find valuable to help them avoid some of the traps we fell into. I would encourage anyone with a dream or a passion to give it a try. You may try and fail, but at least you can live your life knowing you tried. Remember that if you find yourself in a situation where it is not working, you can always make a change. My advice would be to make sure you are seeking God's will and submitting to it. Maybe it will mean starting a company or a not-for-profit someday or maybe it will mean joining others to do big things. Go through the eleven-step process laid out in this book and be willing to go through it again and again when you feel you need an adjustment.

Think of how many people over the last several centuries have ventured to new lands, started new companies, invented new products, and served others in foreign lands. What if they didn't have the passion or the courage to do it when called? The world would be a much less rich and interesting place. We would never discourage someone from starting something new, but would also warn them of the pitfalls and traps so that they would improve their chances of survival. It is not an endeavor for the faint of heart, but it is an incredibly interesting and beautiful journey.

Throughout this time of waiting and transition from Independence Consulting to Point B I have thought of an experience I had many, many years ago when I began in public accounting...

CHAPTER 15

A Long-Range Perspective

The View from Years Ago to the Present

In August of 1992 I set out on an incredible vacation adventure with two of my best friends from work, John O'Connor and Paul Steffens. We were all single, twenty-four years old, and looking for an escape from our work in public accounting. We set out from Charlotte by plane for Boise, Idaho, where we began a four-day whitewater rafting adventure followed by three days hiking in Yellowstone and Grand Teton National Parks. We were about to quickly shift from accountants to true, red-blooded mountain men. Good thing we had trained for the trip—just a hint of sarcasm, as you will see.

We started our trip by entering the Salmon River near Boise. We had chosen our touring company, because they had experts who took the time to teach us techniques. After a few days of instruction, they let us out of the big, guided raft to explore the rapids in single-person, inflatable kayaks.

Each night, after we ate a prepared meal, the guide would map out the next day's rapids in the sand and tell us where we needed to be when we entered each run. The diagrams were detailed—avoid this eddy here, do not hit this rapid over there. The guide's instructions always included pointing out the most dangerous places and what to do if you accidently ended up in that area. I remember dreaming later each night about the details of what was covered in these game-planning sessions. They produced some anxiety, which led to good preparedness. We paid attention during these sessions.

After spending four days rafting and kayaking Class III and Class IV rapids and sleeping in tents on the side of the river we were exhausted. Yet this had been a great experience as we encountered and overcame Class III and Class IV rapids that are described on the internet in the International Scale of River Difficulty as "Intense, powerful but predictable requiring precise boat handling with risk of injury to swimmers that is moderate to high."[10] The scale was created by the American Whitewater Association to evaluate rivers throughout the world, hence *international* in the title.

Then we spent the tail end of the trip in Yellowstone National Park, hiking a very rugged trail. We had flown there on a single-engine Cessna that had seen many years of wilderness flights and landings—more on that later.

John had planned our itinerary well, and we had few glitches. However, we didn't arrive at the Ranger Station at Yellowstone Park until 4:00 P.M. Most people who planned to camp had arrived early in the morning to snag the best campsites. The ranger informed us that all that was left was a campsite called 8M2, thirteen miles from where we would park our rental car. He also told us we would need to hike fast so that we could set up our tents and eat before it was completely dark. He had a very serious face when he said, "You don't want to be on the move after dark with the bears out there."

We wasted little time driving to the parking area, loading our backpacks with all our gear, and setting out down the path. Not only was our hike to our campsite a long thirteen miles, it was also among the least scenic route, snaking through heavily forested areas with few long-range views. We put our heads down and walked fast, setting out around 5:00 P.M. We were tired from the rafting trip and hungry from the long day. It had been a serious workout.

Around 9:00 P.M. we arrived at our campsite, just as the sun was setting. We hurried to get our tents set up, get a fire started, and prepare a delicious meal of freeze-dried meat and veggies! After we inhaled our meal, we made quick preparations for bed, which included packing all our food in bags and hanging them from a pole to keep the food out of reach of bears and other animals. We had been in a hurry, but we definitely remembered the warnings about bears.

We had done our research before leaving on the trip. There are over 800 grizzly bears in Yellowstone, and since 1872 there had been thirty-eight, bear-related injuries to campers and eight fatalities. Bears can grow to a height of seven feet and weigh up to 1,000 pounds. Their sense of smell is better than any animal and 2,100 times better than a human. Bears can smell food from up to twenty miles away. You did not want to invite a bear into your area by leaving trash or food around. I must admit I do believe in preparation, especially when trying something involving risk for the first time. However, as we prepared our three separate tents for bed I kind of wished I hadn't learned so much about bears.

We were all full of the meal and exhausted from the four-day rafting and thirteen-mile speed hike. We had set up each of our one-man tents in a triangle about two yards from each other. We retreated to our respective tents and zipped them up from the inside, ready for a great night's sleep as it was pitch dark now. It did not take me long to start drifting off. (My wife, Kelli, gets so mad at how easily I go to sleep.)

Just as I was drifting into a deep sleep, I heard it. *GRRRRRRRRRRR.* It sounded like a bear beating with its paws on its large chest like King Kong. I couldn't tell for sure, but I thought it was still off in the distance, maybe thirty-to-fifty feet. I was wide awake now with adrenaline flowing through my exhausted body. Survival instincts started kicking in.

"Guys, did you hear that?" I whispered to John and Paul through the thin walls of their nearby tents.

"Yes," they replied in unison.

Without saying a word John and I made it out of our tents and into Paul's. I guess we were thinking there was strength in numbers. We were all pretty big guys, so we were crammed in that single-man tent like the clowns in the tiny car at the circus. Paul was six feet, six inches; John six feet, four inches; and I was the small guy at six feet, zero inches and 185 pounds.

We were in full-blown panic mode as we all huddled together in that tiny tent, contemplating our next move. We knew we were thirteen miles from our car and miles from a Ranger Station. Because we were late to the park we were the furthest campers from help.

I was already imagining the bear ripping through the top of the tent to get to us. No one would even hear us scream so we decided to stay quiet and hope that the bear would walk off. This strategy did not work as we could hear the growling and chest beating sounds getting closer and closer. This went on and on for hours as the bear circled our campsite and at times drew extremely close to our tent.

GRRRRRRRRRRRR, GRRRRRRRRRRRR, the bear roared. This time sounding like it was within feet of our tent. We were terrified and expected to be attacked at any moment. We waited, barely breathing as we expected the bear to come through the tent ceiling. Fear gripped us when we imagined the worst of what would happen next.

Over and over this would repeat itself. The bear would circle the campsite growling and beating its chest as it walked around. There were a few moments where we couldn't hear it, but after only a few minutes the bear would start the process back up again. We didn't dare peak out of the tent, and anyway it was completely pitch dark.

That night none of us got a minute of sleep. The bear stayed at our site from sundown until sun-up the next morning. As first light came through the forest the noises got further and further away until they stopped altogether. Somehow, by the grace of God, we had survived. We poked our heads out of the tent. We were all happy to be alive. "Tired and exhausted" took on a whole new meaning. Despite our exhaustion and lack of sleep we realized we needed to "get out of Dodge." It was thirteen miles back to the car, but we were more than happy to return to civilization.

About halfway into our thirteen-mile hike back to the car, we saw a park ranger in his dark green pants, light-gray, short-sleeve shirt, and "Smokey the Bear" tan hat, standing at the next bend in our trail. As we approached, he said, "Good morning, fellas, how was your night?" as if he knew we were in a hurry to get out for some reason.

"Not great!" I said. "Right after dark as we got in our tents, we heard a bear, and it stayed in our campsite all night long. It did not attack, but it did get close. We did not sleep a wink."

I failed to mention that these three grown men had slept on top of each other in a one-man tent. We had not slept, but we still had a little pride left! That night of "spooning" under the stars would be our little secret (until now of course)!

"What did the bear sound like?" the park ranger asked in a very calm voice.

"Well, it made a growling noise that sounded as if it was beating on its chest like King Kong. It was a low, strong grumbling sound," I explained.

"That's a grouse," he said.

"What's a grouse?" John asked. We had all done our homework, but learned nothing about grouses so we didn't know what he was talking about.

"Well, it's a small bird about the size of a chicken, but plump and fat. It has wings but it's so fat that it just runs around on the ground. It's very slow and you could walk right up to one and punt it like a football if you wanted to—which I'm not advocating, of course!" the ranger replied with a big smile. This was obviously not his first encounter with the dreaded grouse.

John, Paul, and I looked at each other. At first, I don't think we knew whether to laugh or cry. Then one of us cracked and we all belly-laughed until we were doubled over.

As we hiked the remaining six miles we were blessed with a sighting of a small pack of these grouse. There were about eight of them, waddling around. They were, in fact, so slow you could walk right up to them and catch them if you wanted. Strangely, rather than catch one and ring its neck we all walked in circles around them and in between them, laughing and hopping around. We respected the grouse. Their growling was one way they protect themselves from predators at night, making wolves think that a bear is in the area.

This story makes the point that if we don't carefully determine our future and God's purpose for our lives, we might not see clearly and experience God's full purpose. We might see bears rather than grouses.

And we could fear something that isn't really significant.

What are your greatest fears? Is it possible they are grouses?

Name three here:

____

____

____

Have you ever had a fear that once you overcame it, you felt incredible? Mention that here:

____

____

____

Remember that when you are tempted to give in to your fears.

During the process of moving from Independence Consulting I kept having recurring fears of the unknown. Would we pass Point B's due diligence and receive an offer to join their company? Would we have enough funds to survive until we made it to the other side?

Have you ever been in the midst of a trial or feeling like you are stuck in the valley with seemingly insurmountable mountains to climb? Sometime when you are in the valley it is hard to understand why you are going through something and it's difficult to see what good can come from it. It is often only with hindsight and a new higher perspective that you can see how God can use even our greatest struggles to make us better.

Perspectives with Hindsight

Remember that old single-engine Cessna I noted, "More about that later"? Just before we arrived at Yellowstone, we had an amazing journey on that plane that taught me a principle that has stuck with me over twenty-five years.

As we finished our four days and three nights of whitewater rafting and kayaking, John reminded us that we were flying to Yellowstone. He had made the arrangements for this part of the trip, so I was just going with the flow. We were near the last point on the Salmon River so I thought that a car would pick us up and take us to an airport. Nope.

We stood on the edge of the river near a sandy bank that turned to a thin, grassy strip along the river. This part of the river had a nice stretch of riverbank before the canyon walls ascended straight up into the sky. The Salmon River free flows (undammed) 425 miles through mostly untouched wilderness and is considered one of the most beautiful rivers in North America. It is nicknamed "The River of No Return," because of the difficulty experienced by early explorers such as Lewis and Clark trying to cross it or navigate it. The canyon surrounding the Salmon River is the second deepest on the Continent and is 7,000 feet below the highest mountain peak.

Now that we were finished with our kayak tour and had survived and overcome our fears I had a great sense of accomplishment. We unloaded our gear from the boats and the three of us piled our stuff together. Off in the distance, between the canyon walls, I could hear a buzzing sound. Out in the wilderness the sound stuck out as a low humming that echoed far down the river in between the canyon walls. We could hear it before we saw its source.

"Here it comes," said John.

"What?" I asked.

"Our ride, guys," John exclaimed.

Just then we saw a small, single-engine plane emerge from between the canyon walls, flying low over the river. The small plane kept descending to just over the river, then made a gentle landing on a grass strip between the riverbank and the forest, which ascended up the sloping canyon walls. The propeller buzz and engine was loud as it pulled up to within about thirty feet of where we were standing.

Talk about door-to-door service, I thought.

An old man, who looked like he'd been doing this for seventy years, stopped the engine, stepped out, and invited us to immediately load up our gear. As we stowed our packs in the back, I noticed there were exactly four seats. Paul, John, and I were all big guys and with the weight of all our gear I worried a little about takeoff. I couldn't believe it, but had to assume that our pilot would be turning the plane around and taking off from that same narrow strip of grass along the river.

With a concerned smile on his face, our pilot looked at us and said, "You guys are a little bigger than I bargained for. Oh well, jump in and make yourselves comfortable."

We all jumped in and he restarted the engine. This guy was a professional and didn't waste any time getting ready for takeoff. From the back seat I could see the end of the grass runway as it ran directly into the river. We had a short distance to clear the trees on the other side of the river and then ascend quickly to clear the canyon wall. Would our extra weight cause any problems for our aviator?

He cranked up the engine, turned our plane so the nose faced down the grassy stretch, and hit full throttle. Time seemed to slow down as we taxied down the grassy runway, gaining speed. I watched with trepidation as the river's edge approached quickly—with our wheels still touching the ground!

Just as we reached the river, we took flight, only clearing the river by about ten feet. Before I could even think about how close the trees on the other side of the river were, we soared just feet above the tops of the trees and made our way upward. After spending four days on the river, our perspective was different. Most days you would look up and see what seemed like a granite wall of several hundred feet, maybe seven stories tall.

As we reached the canyon peak, I could see another mountain range just beyond the wall. During those four days on the river I thought I'd seen the highest point, but just beyond that first edge was another mountain with a valley in-between. We continued to climb, and our perspective changed. I started to realize why the Salmon River Canyon was the second deepest canyon on the continent. Beyond that next range of mountains, way out in the distance, was another mountain range ever higher than the first. And beyond that another and another and another.

As we got up to our cruising altitude of 13,000 feet, I could see an incredible new perspective. The natural beauty of what God had created overwhelmed me. The four of us crammed in that little tin-can of an airplane now experienced the most breathtaking view. From the lowest point of the river's edge to soaring higher than eagles fly struck me with an imagery that I still remember more than twenty-five years later.

Yet what it meant to me then and what it means to me now are very different. Back then I was amazed by the death-defying experiences and natural beauty. In the two years from that summer in 1992, I would meet Kelli, come to believe in Jesus, experience a spiritual transformation, and marry her on June 11, 1994. I've heard it said, and I now believe, that you can't always appreciate what you are going through in tough times and trials in the moment. Only in hindsight, with a new perspective, can you truly appreciate the good things that come from periods spent in dark valleys. We learn. We get stronger. We can grow closer to our family and closer to God.

Looking back to see the mountains we've climbed and the valleys we have walked through in life gives us a new perspective. But how do we take what we have experienced and apply what we have learned as we move forward? It is important to look back only long enough to inventory the hard-fought lessons. Then it is time to look ahead to the next chapter in our lives and apply our new perspective.

Kelli and I were about to enter our next major period of transition in our lives as we joined Point B. I would experience fear again, I would doubt, but I think this is only human. It may be unavoidable. However, having seen how God brought us through so many trials I would trust him more than any transition period before. He has been teaching me to trust him more and showing me the joy that can be found by doing so.

Over the past twenty years as I've experienced these periods of transition and have shared my advice with friends, clients, and colleagues it has been interesting to see what happens next with people. Only about forty percent take the advice and write their purpose and intentionally describe who they want to be and what they are looking for in life. I always wonder: How can you hit a target if you don't know where you are aiming? My response to this approach is: Go through the steps and intentionally define what your target is.

Will you be one of the sixty percent who continue to flail haphazardly through life or will you be among the forty percent who live their life on purpose, with a mission and the motivation to see something bigger happen with their time on this earth?

Now that you have read *The Guided Journey* I hope you will take the time to complete the steps and write your own unique story. Be intentional about discovering your purpose. This may be the most important assignment of your life.

You were created by God for a special purpose. Share your story and inspire others. Pass it on!

And keep me posted. I can't wait to hear about your journey and what God is doing in your life. Please let me know how you are doing. My email is mikeglee@theguidedjourneybook.com

Bon Voyage, my friend!

AFTERWORD

A New Beginning?

In Chapter Two I described the twists and turns that were part of my spiritual journey. And you have seen how I relied on my faith throughout my years as a business consultant.

Now I'm wondering about you. Are you open to a new beginning?

Maybe you are still hesitant. If you are not ready to submit your life to Jesus at this time, you might think about my journey and how faith was so important to me—and might be an important part of your future.

However, if you are ready to make a commitment to Jesus, walk through this short prayer with me.

Dear Heavenly Father,

I thank you for bringing me to this moment in my life where I am ready to come into a relationship with you through Your Son Jesus. I believe that Jesus came to this earth for me, that he was crucified, bled, and died as a sacrifice for my sins. I believe he was buried in a tomb and after three days he was resurrected and that he is seated at your right hand in heaven. I confess my sins to you, Father, and promise to turn from my current life to a new life with you. From this day forward, I commit my life to you.

If you just prayed that prayer, we have incredible reason to celebrate. You are now beginning a new life in Christ Jesus. Write your name and commitment date in the space below:

Name: ______________________________

Commitment Date:______________________

You are promised an eternity in heaven. Let us praise God from whom all blessing flow.

If you are already a Christian, you might think about your testimony. As a believer you have a story to tell. And it's unique. The stories of how people come to a relationship with God are as many and as varied as the millions of people who have come to a saving faith. The solution in Jesus is the same, but how we get there is so different, and no two people's stories are the same. God, our Creator, Creator of Heaven and Earth, finds us in our own unique and special way. What is your testimony? What will your testimony be?

Take a moment now to jot down what that testimony might involve.

____

____

____

____

Then over the next weeks, write your complete testimony—and be ready to share it. You might be the catalyst for someone to make a commitment that will change his or her life forever.

And ask yourself this question: How can God use me to build his kingdom in heaven and on earth? What is my mission field? It took me years to realize that my mission field was not as a pastor, but to reach people through my work in consulting, by being a faith-led business person, and by being a present coach, mentor, and friend to my clients and colleagues. Helping them discover their God-given purpose in life.

In those moments when I was lost in darkness and frustrated or even exasperated at my own failed efforts, it was My God, My Jesus, and My Holy Spirit, who found me and led me out. Most importantly, the perfect Word of God has been a reliable source of truth and direction in all these moments and throughout my life. I only wish I had gone there earlier and more often. I'm grateful that in my weakest and worst moments my God was strong and capable to carry and lead me out. It is not something I did. It is what he did for me—100 percent.

Don't settle for anything less than the best God has planned for you. Open your heart and your mind to the incredible possibilities. Give your life to the Creator of everything. He loves you so much and wants to use you to do big things during your time here on earth. Dream Big! No matter where you've been or what you've done he can redeem it all and do incredible things through you if you will let him take control. If you have been bored or unsatisfied with your own efforts, give God a chance to reshape your life.

Close your eyes and think about sailing to a new destination. Get into that boat with Jesus and you will not be disappointed. This will be an epic journey. God wants me to tell you that your life matters dearly to him. You will not be alone. He will go with you wherever you go. I pray especially that you will find that "fire in your belly."

All proceeds I receive from the publication of this book will be donated to www.onebyonecostarica.com.

ACKNOWLEDGMENTS

I thank God for laying the idea of this book on my heart. I thank Pastor Padilla who helped me see the vision God had for *The Guided Journey*. When Pastor shared his message from God—you are supposed to write a book to share what God has done in your life— my first thought was one I'm not proud to admit. I asked Pastor Padilla this question, "How can I write a book when I need to focus my time, energy, and resources on getting this consulting business off the ground—especially after I suffered the brain injury five months ago and have only been fully recovered for two months?"

Pastor Padilla immediately replied, "Michael, God will provide you the time and the resources you need in his timing—not yours. You don't need to worry about when it is complete, just commit to doing the work." So, it's not surprising that God has provided everything needed.

I'm thankful for Janet Thoma, my book coach and editor, who guided me through every step of the process from the original idea of the book, our thesis statement, the outline, and finding a publisher. Pat Williams, senior vice president of the NBA's Orlando Magic, nicknamed her "the piranha" when she worked with him on several books. Janet will tell you when something isn't high quality, doesn't make sense, or needs to be thrown in the garbage. I so appreciate her for this. I thank one of my best friends Stuart Stout for introducing me to Janet. She has been a God-send. I could not have done this without her. Or her son-in-law, Jim Wilke, who formatted the book for typesetting.

Kathryn Helmers of Creative Trust was instrumental in introducing us to the innovative team at Morgan James Publishing. Thank you, David Hancock for believing in this project and enabling us to bring it to market.

I also thank Kelli and my kids for their belief in me and patience as I pursued another "crazy" God-inspired project.

I hope this book is a great gift to you and your family. I pray for incredible things for your journey through life.

ABOUT THE AUTHOR

Mike Lee is an executive with Point B, an integrated management consulting, digital services, venture investment, and real-estate development firm. He is the former founder and president of Independence Consulting and former president of North Highland Worldwide Consulting. With significant experience leading high-level consulting firms, this is the third business he has helped build.

As the former president of North Highland, a global consulting firm with more than 1,200 professionals in twenty-five cities around the world, Mike was a key driver of North Highland's international expansion and Cordence Worldwide partnerships. He was directly responsible for North Highland's United States, United Kingdom, and China operations and led the firm's efforts to globally deliver deep-industry expertise across all markets and clients.

Mike has twenty-five plus years of experience in business transformation for Fortune 500 companies and Public Sector businesses. His specific areas of expertise include strategic planning, finance, and HR function development, process improvement, and enterprise resource planning systems. Mike has served the financial services, media, life sciences, retail, manufacturing, distribution, and utilities industries, managing strategic planning, mergers and acquisitions, cost and efficiency programs, product development, and shared services engagements.

Mike joined North Highland in 2003 and played an instrumental role in the growth of the company from $40M in revenue to over $400M in 2015. Prior to being named president, he served as EVP, starting and running the firm's second largest office in Charlotte, North Carolina, opening new U.S. offices, and assisting with international expansion.

Before joining North Highland, Mike was employed for thirteen years with Arthur Andersen Business Consulting where he was promoted to partner two weeks before the Enron scandal broke, which led to that firm's historic collapse. Prior to that, Mike was a managing director at BearingPoint. He holds a bachelor's degree from Virginia Tech with a major in accounting. Mike is an inactive CPA.

ENDNOTES

1 The Living Bible

2 Psalm 118:24, King James Version

3 New King James Version

4 Francis Frangipane, *The Three Battlegrounds* (Cedar Rapids, Idaho, Arrow Publications, Inc., 2012). 28.

5 Paul Fraisse, "Perception and Estimation of Time," *Annual Review Psychology* (Paris, France, Annual Reviews, Inc., 1984), Issue 35, 10.

6 1 Samuel 15: 22-23b, New Living Translation

7 New King James Version

8 Proverbs 3:6, NKJ

9 Romans 8:28, KJV

10 *International Scale of River Difficulty*, American Whitewater, www.americanwhitewater.org.

Printed in the USA
CPSIA information can be obtained
at www.ICGtesting.com
JSHW022332140824
68134JS00019B/1430